Personality and Sense of Humor

Avner Ziv received his Ph.D. in clinical psychology from the Sorbonne in Paris. Since 1981, Professor Ziv has been chairman of the Department of Educational Sciences at Tel Aviv University. He served as coordinator of the Graduate Program of Educational Psychology at Bar Ilan University and the counseling program at Tel Aviv University. As visiting professor, he taught at Boston University and at the University of Quebec in Montreal. He was one of the founding members of the International Society for the study of groups in Paris and president of the Educational Psychology Division of the Israeli Psychological Association. In addition to his frequent contribution to the professional literature in American, British, French, and Hebrew journals, he has published ten books which have been translated into six languages, including *Humor in Education: A Psychological Approach, The Psychology of Humor, Counseling the Intellectually Gifted Child, Psychology in Education* and *Adolescence*. Dr. Ziv is the chairman of the forthcoming Fourth International Conference on Humor and the First International Colloquium on Jewish Humor.

Personality and Sense of Humor

Avner Ziv, Ph.D.

SPRINGER PUBLISHING COMPANY
New York

Springer Publishing Company, Inc.
200 Park Avenue South
New York, New York 10003

84 85 86 87 88 / 10 9 8 7 6 5 4 3 2 1

Library of Congress Cataloging in Publication Data

Ziv, Avner.
  Personality and sense of humor.
  Bibliography: p.   Includes index.
  1. Wit and humor—Psychological aspects. 2. Personality. I. Title.
BF575.L3Z58   1984   152.4   84–1372
ISBN 0–8261–4540–X

Printed in the United States of America
Illustrations by François Labelle

Most people I love have one thing
in common: a good sense of humor.
To them, who helped me not only to
cope better with life's difficulties
but also to enjoy it more, this
book is dedicated — with love and humor.

Contents

Introduction

Laughter is an intriguing phenomenon. It is a daily occurrence, clearly visible and audible. At the turn of the century, Dearborn gave a very precise description of laughter:

> There occur in laughter and more or less in smiling, clonic spasms of the diaphragm[,] in number ordinarily about eighteen perhaps, and contraction of most of the muscles of the face. The upper side of the mouth and its corners are drawn upward. The upper eyelid is elevated, as are also, to some extent, the brows, the skin over the glabella, and the upper lip, while the skin at the outer canthi of the eyes is characteristically puckered. The nostrils are moderately dilated and drawn upward, the tongue slightly extended, and the cheeks distended and drawn somewhat upward; in persons with the pinnal muscles largely developed, the pinnae tend to incline forwards. The lower jaw vibrates or is somewhat withdrawn (doubtless to afford all possible air to the distending lungs), and the head, in extreme laughter, is thrown backward; the trunk is straightened even to the beginning of bending backward, until (and this usually happens soon), fatigue-pain in the diaphragm and accessory abdominal muscles causes a marked proper flexion of the trunk for its relief. The whole arterial vascular system is dilated, with consequent blushing from the effect on the dermal capillaries of the face and neck, and at times the scalp and hands. From this same cause[,] in the main[,] the eyes often slightly bulge forwards and the lachrymal gland becomes active, ordinarily to a degree only to cause a "brightening" of the eyes, but often to such an extent that the tears overflow entirely their proper channels. (1900, p. 853)

But what makes people laugh?

Laughter being so evidently physical, one might be tempted to guess that it is produced by physical stimuli. Indeed, in some cases it is. We all know the technique of tickling a person to induce laughter. But it is not so simple, as you can easily discover through a simple experiment: Try tickling yourself. You didn't laugh, did you? It appears that something is missing. Tickling, like loving, requires two partners.

A second experiment can be thought about, but I do not recommend actually carrying it out. Imagine going up to a stranger in the street and tickling him. It is not very likely that the stranger would laugh; more probably he would be frightened and would want to escape. This means that the partners in a tickling process need to feel secure with each other. Children laugh when tickled by their parents, but not when strangers try to tickle them. It seems, therefore, that even in such a simple laughing situation as tickling, a social relationship has to be involved — and not just any social relationship, but a positive one.

Laughter induces pleasurable emotional states. Generally, although not always, one may infer on observing a person laughing that he feels enjoyment (as one can infer from a person's crying that he feels sadness). We should also bear in mind that laughter is more often caused by words and symbols — by jokes and cartoons, for example — than by physical acts; jokes, of course, provide intellectual rather than physical stimulation.

Thus laughter is an extremely complex phenomenon that possesses physiological, social, emotional, and intellectual aspects; these aspects cover the entire area of psychology. But what, in fact, causes laughter? Since Plato, philosophers, writers, and even humorists have proposed a multitude of theories. Over 100 were described by Gregory in 1924. One of the main causes of laughter is humor. As opposed to *laughter,* which is easily observable and can be described with precision, *humor* is an elusive concept. Humorous activities have many labels. Something can be funny, amusing, droll, comic, absurd, laughable, mirth-provoking, or ludicrous. A person can have a sense of humor or can be a wit, a joker, a funny man, a jester, a buffoon, a clown, or a humorist.

The many efforts to define humor have not been very successful. In a popular book entitled *L'Humour (Humor),* Robert Escarpit (1963) tried to do so, but the title of the first chapter is "On the Impossibility of Defining Humor," and from there on he struggles with the problem. It may seem strange that something so common should present such a difficulty. People intuitively "know" what humor is. They have no problem in pointing out which of their friends have a good sense of humor and which are dull and humorless. Later in this book, it becomes clear that even young children "know" the meaning of humor. Nevertheless, the difficulties of definition do exist, mainly because we refer to humor in its different forms as if it were a unitary concept.

In fact, there are two main dimensions to be considered when one studies humor: the ability to appreciate it, and the ability to create it. The two are of course related in some ways, but they also differ. Let me explain briefly what I mean by these two dimensions. *Humor creativity* refers to the ability to perceive relationships between people, objects, or ideas in an incongruous way, as well as the ability to communicate this perception to others. The communication can be verbal or nonverbal, and it elicits smiling or laughter. *Humor appreciation* refers to the ability to understand and enjoy messages involving humorous creativity, as well as situations that are incongruous but not menacing.

I discuss these two dimensions in more detail later on. When we speak of a person's having "a good sense of humor," we sometimes mean that the person possesses a well-developed appreciation of humor and sometimes that he has a creative flair for it. And sometimes, of course, we mean both. For the time being, let us use these definitions of the two main dimensions of humor in order to agree on what we are talking about when we say "humor."

But why is it that what is humorous to some does not seem so to others? There is nothing universal about humor appreciation. Any given joke will probably amuse some people and bore others. And as to humor creativity, what sorts of people are blessed with such talent, and what differentiates them from those who lack it? This book tries to elucidate these questions and to offer some answers—to illuminate, that is to say, the relation between humor and personality.

In Parts I and II of this book, the central issues relating to humor are dealt with. These can be formulated as questions:

1. *Why* do people create and enjoy humor? What purposes does it serve? In other words, what are its psychological *functions?*

2. *How* is humor made? What are the *techniques* used in creating and enjoying it?

3. *What* is the subject matter of humor? What *topics* can it deal with?

4. *Where* does humor appear most frequently? What are the *situations* that enhance or reduce it?

The main functions of humor (question 1) are discussed in Part I of the book; the issues of technique, topic, and situation (questions 2–4) are discussed in Part II.

Part III of the book concentrates on the two dimensions of appreciation and creativity and their relation to personality — the "Who?" of humor. A theory of personality is first briefly outlined, taking into account its emotional, social, and intellectual aspects. Then I explain which sorts of personalities appreciate what kinds of humor, relating personality to the theoretical aspects of humor presented in Parts I and II. Finally, I discuss the personality of a humorist. A *humorist* is a person who creates humor, either professionally or only occasionally (an "amateur").

A few words are in order concerning the way in which the text is presented. Jokes and cartoons now and then illustrate the themes introduced. It would be sad to write a book on humor without offering at least a little of it. Concerning the jokes, I do not pretend that they are new or original. They are simply good — as far as my own personality allows me to judge jokes. I like them, and I hope that my readers will too. They are printed in italics so that those who are interested only in the "serious" aspects of the subject can ignore them. (Of course, those who love jokes can read just them and — God forbid! — ignore the text.) The cartoons were drawn by my colleague François Labelle of the University of Quebec in Montreal, where I spent a sabbatical year. François is one of those rare psychologists who, in addition to his love for and interest in our discipline, is also blessed with a wonderful sense of humor and a splendid creative graphic talent. While in Montreal I discussed my ideas with him, and he rapidly produced these drawings. They are original and intelligent, and I hope the reader will enjoy them as much as I do.

Now and then, "Examples" are used to present some ideas in detail or to display research designs or results. The involved reader may find them of interest, but others can follow the text without consulting them.

Parts I and II of the book are largely theoretical. Part III is based mostly on original research and includes excerpts from interviews with professional and amateur humorists. I have tried to avoid psychological jargon as much as I can; this is because I believe that interest in humor is not restricted to psychologists only. I firmly hold that psychological investigation can be presented to nonpsychologists in understandable language. However, I also hope that psychologists and other research-oriented professionals will be inspired to continue, to verify, and to get more involved in research related to humor. I can assure them that this is a fascinating area, one in which research methods can be applied and in which inventive approaches are needed. In addition, unlike the subjects of most research in psychology, the subjects of humor-related research enjoy the process themselves. It is a great experience to work in research and hear the subjects laugh as they undergo tests.

When working on this book, I initially intended to outline the principal theories of humor, but since the interested reader can find many such reviews, I rapidly changed my mind. When necessary, what are from my point of view the three most important theories are cited but not described in detail. These are the theories proposed by Freud, in *Jokes and their Relation to the Unconsciousness* (1905/1916); by Bergson, in *Le Rire (Laughter)* (1899/1975); and by Koestler, whose *The Act of Creation* (1964) focuses on humor in its first section. Any reader who is really interested in humor should read these books.

It is more enjoyable to read a humorous book than to read one explaining humor. However, I do hope that a better understanding of humor can make it more enjoyable. I hope that the jokes and cartoons illustrating points I wish to emphasize will help to make the reading more pleasurable.

I

THE FUNCTIONS
OF HUMOR

Psychologists do not agree among themselves on most concepts related to human behavior. One notable exception is the idea that all behavior is motivated. People do things for reasons. There is always *at least* one motivation behind every behavior.

Laughter is a daily occurrence for most of us. One study even pointed out that American students laugh on the average 16 times a day. As I have pointed out, laughter generally accompanies pleasurable emotional states. Humans, being pleasure-seeking animals, therefore try to create situations that provoke laughter. This is the main motivation for humorous situations. Such situations can be verbal (as in jokes or comedies), visual (as in cartoons or slapstick), and even musical. But why are certain situations laughter-provoking?

Among the numerous theories proposed, one can find some that accentuate humor techniques. Others focus on the situations in which humor appears or on the contents of humorous messages. However, most theories concentrate on what humor does to people. Every theory illuminates one facet of what humor does for us. Each one can illustrate its main point by presenting numerous examples. "Jokes that fit the theory" are luckily abundant, because humor deals with everything human. However each author presenting a theory has the very human tendency to see the jokes that fit the theory's main points and to ignore those that do not. This can be nicely illustrated by a short anecdote used by a famous Hungarian humorist, Karinty Frigyes (1937), as an introduction to one of his books.

> *During target-shooting exercises, the sergeant loses his patience. None of the recruits are succeeding in hitting the target. He snatches a rifle from one of the recruits and shouts, "Now watch me." He aims carefully, shoots, and misses. In the tense silence, the sergeant doesn't lose his cool. "You see," he turns to*

1

one of the recruits, "that's how you shoot." He aims again, shoots, and misses again. He turns to another recruit: "And that's how you shoot." Again the sergeant loads his rifle, aims, and fires, with the same result and the same comment. Finally he hits the target, and, beamingly, he tells his soldiers, "You see, this is how I shoot."

Of course it is easier to criticize a theory than to create one. It is not my intention to find faults in the existing theories, but rather to integrate them. Humor is too complex a phenomenon to be explained by one particular approach.

In my view, humor is created and enjoyed because it allows us to do many things that we need to do—to express fundamental needs in ways that are not only pleasurable (because accompanied by laughter or smiling), but also socially accepted and valued. What needs can humor fulfill?

First, it deals with social taboos. When analyzing the content of jokes, one finds that most deal with aggression and sex. These topics also happen to be two of the main taboos of our society. Aggression is probably part of human nature, whether we like it or not. A look at humanity's history would be sufficient to convince anyone. However, in order to keep society functioning, aggression has to be regulated and controlled; each society allows the expression of aggressive needs in special ways. One example is the wonderful world of competitive sports. A look at a boxing match can be quite revealing. Boxing, also named "the noble sport" (probably by someone with a good sense of humor), has the following scenario: Two people, well trained, hit each other as hard as they can after shaking hands and putting on gloves. The spectators, civilized and well-behaved people who chat nicely with their neighbors, change their behavior as soon as the gong signals the beginning of the match. Then they start shouting, giving good advice to the fighters (such as "Kill him!"), gesticulating, and howling their approval when one boxer or the other bleeds and falls down. After the match, the fighters leave the ring (alone or carried), and the spectators, exhausted but with shining eyes, return to their homes and to civilized behavior. Sports are just one example of the expression of aggression in a socially acceptable way. There are many others (such as literary criticism), and humor is one of them. Some authors believe that all humor is aggressive and that its main function is just this: to allow people to express and enjoy aggression in a socially approved manner.

The other social taboo with which humor allows us to deal openly is sexuality. In spite of the sexual revolution, sex creates many problems, and it is a fascinating topic for most of us. Humor allows us to deal with it and to derive some pleasure from it vicariously without encountering too much social censure. As becomes clear in Chapter 2, the lessening of sexual taboos creates some different problems, and humor allows us to tackle them in a pleasurable manner.

A third function of humor is the social one. Humor can be a way of improving society. Social criticism in the form of satire is one way of trying to change things for the better. Humor used in satire is generally of an aggressive type, but its main function is social. Another aspect of the social function of humor is related to interaction in groups. Humor can be used to achieve social acceptance, to gain status, and to reinforce group cohesiveness. It can oil the wheels of face-to-face relations, but it can also pour sand in them. Most humor appears and blossoms among friends, and it strengthens positive relations.

Negative aspects of our life, our fears and anxieties, dominate many of our thoughts. Yet another of the functions of humor is to deal with anxieties as a defense mechanism. Laughing at things that frighten us makes them less menacing. "Gallows humor" or "black humor" pokes fun at illness, death, and other fear-evoking topics. As a defense mechanism, humor is even used against ourselves; self-disparagement is considered the "highest" form of humor by some.

Finally, the fifth function of humor is an intellectual one. Using humor to escape for a short while from the bondage of rationality fulfills a need we all feel from time to time. Exercising our intellectual capacities to solve problems in a pleasurable way is part of the intellectual function of humor.

In the first part of this book, I discuss these five functions of humor. Most forms of humor fulfill one or more of these functions. Possibly one can find types of humor that have functions different from these, but they are rare exceptions. I begin in Chapter 1 with the aggressive functions of humor.

1

The Aggressive Function
of Humor

The savage who cracked his enemy over the head with a tomahawk and
shouted "Ha, Ha" was the first humorist.

— Stephen Leacock

EARLY THEORIES OF HUMOR AS AGGRESSION

As an expression of aggression, humor has a long history. If we count
the number of times the word "laugh" appears in the Bible, we find
29 instances, in 13 of which (45%) there is an aggressive connotation.
So Jeremiah finds himself attacked: "O Lord, Thou hast enticed me,
and I was enticed; Thou hast overcome me and hast prevailed; I am
become a laughing stock all the day, every one mocketh me" (Jeremiah 20:7).

The Greeks were the first to try to understand laughter and its
essence. Plato wrote that people laugh when they come across a weakness in another person, the laughter being an attack on the weakness
and indirectly on the person. Aristotle explained laughter as the pleasure of humiliating and belittling someone else. The fact that someone
is funny also makes that person ridiculous, ugly, and repulsive. These
two opinions have had a great influence upon the comprehension of
the essence of humor. To this day, the basic theory of Plato and Aristotle is fairly popular. The British humorist Mikes (1970) insists, "All
humor is aggressive."

The great power of humorous expression emerges in a story told
about the Greek poet Archilochus, the originator of the iambic meter.

4

He was born to a maidservant and a priest. When he came of age, he wanted to marry a girl from a distinguished family, whose father initially consented; however, on discovering the origin of his future son-in-law, the father refused to let the marriage take place. The raging Archilochus wrote a satirical poem (in iambs, of course) about the father and daughter and read it in front of an audience in the theater. On the following day the father and daughter, their honor destroyed by their having become laughingstocks of the community, committed suicide. This story, which is believed to be true, may lead us to give a second thought to the truth of the famous French saying, *Le ridicule ne tue pas* (Ridicule doesn't kill).

The Arabs resemble the Greeks in their comprehension of humor as a dangerous and destructive weapon. In the Middle Ages, Arab tribes went to war accompanied by a satirist. In his book on satire, Highet (1954) tells how one Arab satirist would compose humorous poetry *(Hidja)* on the eve of a battle. It was directed against the enemy, depicting the tribe and its leader as ridiculous and weak. This satire was recited during the moments of confrontation, the satirist being positioned among the fighters in the front lines and throwing out his remarks in the face of the enemy, whose morale was seriously affected by this attack. When the tribe prevailed, the witty songwriter was decorated, just as the bravest warriors were.

This story shows us that the Arabs thought of humor as an aggressive weapon and were aware of its mighty powers. The combat of laughter and sword also appears in the mythology of the Australian tribe of Bendar (Brown, 1925). Bindlain, the chief of the tribe, had two wives. They made his life miserable until he couldn't stand it any more, so one day he got rid of them in the surest and most final way. But his wives had two brothers, and he feared their revenge. From that day on, he kept his sword by his side. The brothers knew that they would have to trick it away from him. One night, when the members of the tribe were gathered around a campfire, the brothers put on such a funny act that Bindlain rolled around with laughter and left his sword for a moment. At that moment they pounced on him, stabbed him to death, and threw him into the fire.

Philosophers of our day and age continue to discuss laughter and humor and to recognize the aggressive element in both. Why should so much attention be given to this?

THE DEVELOPMENT OF AGGRESSIVE HUMOR: RAPP'S THEORY

Aggression is part of the essence of the human race. It seeks out avenues of expression — if possible, in a direct form, but more commonly in indirect form. Among these indirect forms, humor plays an important part. In order to understand this, we must first understand what aggression is and what its sources are.

Rapp (1949) is among the psychologists who have claimed that aggression is an instinct and that humor is one of its modes of expression. In 1949 he proposed a theory of the development of humor as an aggressive expression, connecting it with the physical aggression of primitive man and claiming that laughter first appeared in warfare. At the end of the battle, the victor would relieve his tension with a vocal "Ha . . . ha . . . ha." The loser would relieve his tension by crying. And so laughter came to symbolize victory. In addition to his tears, the loser was usually swollen and covered with bruises, looking grotesque. When people laughed at these outward signs of losing, they were actually identifying with the winner. This is how humor directed against losers came into being. A more modern version of this theory is elegantly described in Gruner's excellent book *Understanding Laughter* (1978).

With the evolution of civilization, intellectual warfare began to replace physical warfare: Words were exchanged instead of blows. The intellect has proven to be a dangerous weapon. In the first stage, the same rules as in physical warfare are in effect: Each side strives for victory. This is apparent in guessing competitions. Questions are asked; the one who guesses correctly is the winner, and the other is the loser. The winner laughs, and the loser is sad. Guessing confrontations of this sort are to be found in the Greek, Egyptian, and Scandinavian mythologies. The Sphinx, for example, would ask passers-by, "What walks on four legs in the morning, on two at noon, and on three at night?" Those who could not guess were immediately killed. One day Oedipus (later to be well known in psychoanalysis) found the answer. When the Sphinx heard it, she committed suicide.

A joke competition is a primitive form of humor enjoyed mainly by children. One child may ask another, "Why did the chicken cross the road?" After a few attempts at guessing, the second child is asked, "Give up?" If he answers affirmatively he admits to defeat, and the winner (the child who asked the riddle) explains, "To get to the other side." The reader very probably is not laughing at this, but young children rarely fail to enjoy it. The amusement is caused by one of the basic techniques of humor: surprise.

The relatively primitive humor in a riddle or guessing game takes on a more sophisticated form in humorous remarks. In such remarks aggression is hidden, but it exists.

This, in outline, is Rapp's theory about the development of aggressive humor from physical battle to irritating remarks. Aggressive behavior takes on many forms. The instinctive impulse is enriched by learning processes, and different theories have stressed the learning aspect of aggression. Adler's theory emphasizes the universality of inferiority feelings, while the classical theory of frustration and aggression has been put forward by Dollard and Miller (1939).

AGGRESSIVE HUMOR: A WAY TO ACHIEVE SUPERIORITY

Adler's theory concentrates mainly on the dynamic aspect of the personality and man's never-ending effort to hide his feelings of inferiority. The inferiority complex, as Adler sees it, is part of the normal development process of every human being. A child grows and develops in an environment where adults impress him with their size, voices, and personalities. He sees them as being able to do anything and everything, and when he compares himself with them he cannot help feeling inferior. Therefore the main motive of human behavior is the constant effort to cover up the feelings of inferiority implanted in us from an early age. We compensate for these feelings by trying to achieve and prove superiority in one field or another.

Like all theories, Adler's can be supported by examples throughout history. Demosthenes, for example, worked hard in order to overcome the inferiority complex that was an outcome of his stuttering from birth. He eventually became a great orator and emphasized his superiority in the exact area in which he was inferior to begin with.

Adler raised the inferiority complex to the status of a universal explanation for all human behavior. Even if we reject this approach as too radical, there is no doubt that a sense of inferiority is a component of human nature, and one that causes a person to take action in order to prove in himself a degree of superiority. The ways in which man attempts this are many. He may condemn himself to strenuous and long-range work in order to excel in a certain area. Being awarded a Nobel Prize crowns a scientist's efforts and proves his superiority over his colleagues. But it is possible to achieve a feeling of superiority in a way that requires much less effort — namely, by merely detracting from the superiority of others. When we succeed in reducing someone's power or status, it is as if we have elevated ourselves in comparison with him. Although the superior feeling is imaginary and momentary, it is enjoyable. Humor that points its arrows at a person of high position is actually an expression of aggression toward him. However, humor has a way of disguising its aggression, so that we are not always aware of its hostile element and think that we are only enjoying its sharp-wittedness.

In his treatise on human nature (1650), Hobbes defined *laughter* as "nothing but the sudden glory arising from some sudden conception of some eminence in ourselves, by comparison with the infirmity of others, or with our own formerly."

Folklore is rich with mockery of the hero and portrayal of him as a fool. We respond to this sort of humor because in comparison with the wise men of Gotham of the Yiddish folk tales, for example, we can all be considered Einsteins, and there is no doubt about our superiority. The following story belongs to this category of humor:

> *Mother sends Herschel Ostropotiev [the Yiddish folk fool] to buy matches. When he returns, she tries to light them, but to no avail. "What's this?" she says angrily. "All the matches are duds." "How can that be?" answers Herschel. "I tested every one of them myself."*

In comparison with Herschel, who would not feel himself a wise man? Here is another example:

> *After their boat has sunk, two friends float for days holding on to a tree trunk. Suddenly, they spot dry land. One of them starts swimming towards it, ignoring the other's cries that he can't swim. On reaching the shore, he turns around on the sand and dives back into the water in order to rescue his friend. Clinging to him, the friend asks, "But why did you leave me all alone?" He answers, "I had to save myself first in order to be able to save you!"*

In these two jokes we have the opportunity to attack foolish behavior and laugh at it. Emphasizing the stupidity of the joke's hero
gives us a sense of superiority: "Compared to him, even I'm a genius!"

Aggressive humor motivated by the need to feel superior does
not only attack characters who excel in stupidity. It also enables us
to express hostility toward our equals or even those above us, those
of greater status. Here is an example:

> Bernard Shaw sent Churchill a ticket to the premiere of one of his
> plays with a note: "I'd be glad to see you among the audience."
> Churchill returned the ticket with a note of his own: "I apologize for
> not being able to attend the premiere. I will gladly come to a later
> night, if there is one." Shaw then sent him two tickets for another eve-
> ning and wrote, "I'll be glad if you come to the show accompanied by a
> friend, if you have one."

Another example is the story told about de Gaulle (or any other
politician of the reader's choice):

> de Gaulle and his wife are sitting in their living room. He's reading
> and she is knitting. "Oh God," says his wife, "it's so cold." de Gaulle
> turns to her and says, "When we're alone, you can call me Charles."

In such ways does humor fulfill its aggressive role and give us
a sense of momentary but enjoyable superiority. In addition, it also
enables us to take revenge on those who frustrate us. A sense of frustration is produced when we come across an obstacle that prevents
us from achieving important goals. When other people are the sources
of frustration, there is a tendency to react aggressively toward them.
This is the basis of a theory of frustration and aggression developed
by Dollard and Miller in 1939.

Dollard and Miller's theory explains why frustration is one of the
main reasons for aggressive behavior. Frustration is a psychological
feeling accompanied by physiological tension that is aroused when ob-
stacles appear in the way of a personal goal. The psychological and
physiological tension of frustration causes us to seek its discharge,
which in most cases takes the form of aggressive behavior. This aggressiveness is directed either against objects or — more frequently —
against persons who cause frustrations.

Who frustrates us? Who doesn't? For children, sources of frustration include parents, teachers, older brothers and sisters, and other children. For adults, almost anyone we have contact with can be a cause of frustration. This is particularly true in regard to those whose job or position enables them to dictate what we can or cannot do. Judges, doctors, clerks, government officials — all these are attractive targets for humor's arrows, which bring them down from their superior position and give us revenge for their frustrating us or being able to frustrate us. Since direct aggression against frustrating individuals or groups is not permitted in our society, it generally takes hidden forms. Humor is one. It allows us to express aggressive feelings in a socially accepted way.

Aggressive humor takes on many forms, from a direct and insulting attack to a clever and gentle play on words. These can be shown within a theoretical framework that helps us to understand the dimensions of aggressive humor. The first dimension is that of the victim, against which the humor is directed; the second is that of the form in which the humor is expressed. Figure 1.1 presents the approach

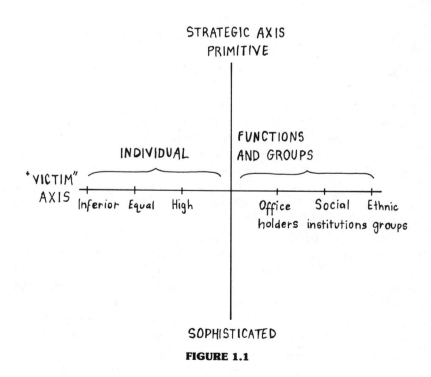

FIGURE 1.1

schematically. The horizontal axis represents the victim of aggression; the left-hand side refers to individuals, and the right-hand side refers to groups or to those who hold high official positions. The left-hand side indicates the relationship between the creator of humor and his victim as an individual. Usually the victim is a person who is constantly degraded and ridiculed. The sort of humor that stresses someone's stupidity, and in so doing makes him inferior, can be considered within this category. Such victims include the village fool, a maidservant, a delivery boy, or the "Herschel" mentioned earlier. Then comes the sort of humor aimed at offending a person equal in status to oneself—a friend or a colleague. The last position on the left-hand side of the axis is the victim whose status is higher than the humorist's: a teacher in relation to a pupil, a boss in relation to an employee, or simply a parent in relation to a child. (See Example 1.1.) The doctor is a familiar victim of this type:

> *A doctor fills out a death certificate and signs his name under the heading "Cause of Death."*

The psychiatrist is even more familiar:

> *A doctor visits a friend and finds him in a state of progressive hysteria, shouting in a frenzy, "I can't stand it any more, I have to see a psychiatrist."*
> *"But you are a psychiatrist," says the doctor.*
> *"I know, but I'm too expensive."*

The judge is another common "superior" victim:

> *At the end of a trial for assault and robbery, the judge enters the courtroom and says to the accused, "I find you to be innocent." The accused jumps with joy and says to the judge, "That's terrific! Does that mean I can keep the money?"*

To this list we can add teachers, clergymen, clerks, and others, moving along toward the right on the horizontal axis until we come to the various social institutions. No government can escape being a target for the aggressive humor of its subjects, especially the talented ones among them—the satirists. Political parties receive similar treat-

---

EXAMPLE 1.1
The Suffering of Authority Figures Amuses Us

Cantor and Zillman (1973) wished to verify whether aggression aimed at those who possess authority is more amusing than aggression aimed at someone of similar status. A group of 76 psychology students was presented with a series of cartoons. In some the victim held a position of authority (banker, policeman, etc.); in others he was an ordinary person, similar to the participants (student, guitar player, etc.). All the cartoons suggested that something unpleasant was about to happen to the victim. In every case, the assailant was either an animal or a child. The students were asked to rate the cartoons according to their facetiousness.

Analysis of the results showed that the cartoons in which the victims held a position of authority were considered funnier than the others. The researchers came to the conclusion that the results supported Hobbes' hypothesis: Our need to feel superior is stronger when a person who possesses high authority and a higher position than our own is in question.

---

ment, and so do holy institutions like marriage. Alexandre Dumas once wrote, for example,

> *The strains of marriage are so heavy that it takes two to carry them, sometimes even three.*

At the extreme right-hand end of the horizontal axis is the aggressive humor aimed at ethnic groups. In this category come jokes about the Irish, the Polish, the Scots, and so on. Jews in the Diaspora have always fallen victim to many forms of aggressive ethnic humor. The fact that in Israel Jews from one community choose Jews from another one as victims can raise some sad thoughts about man's strong need to prove his superiority by finding a group that can be ridiculed.

The horizontal axis of Figure 1.1 refers to the victim of aggressive humor, who is generally external to the creator of the humor. There is a form of aggressive humor in which the creator himself is the victim; he ridicules himself and tells others of his ridiculous characteristics. Such self-disparaging humor is rare. More is said on the matter in the discussion of humor as a defense mechanism in Chapter 4.

The vertical axis of Figure 1.1 refers to the manner in which the humorous attack is expressed. It describes an assortment of strategies, beginning with direct, primitive aggression and ending with sophisticated and well-hidden aggression.

What is meant by a "primitive" approach is an open and crude attack in which the humor is rather thin. As we move down the vertical axis, we come across more refined approaches. In a hidden attack, the humorous covering is so effective that the attack hardly registers as such.

For years a variegated industry has supplied players of practical jokes with an apparatus for secret attacks devoid of humorous talent: flowers that spurt water up a person's nose as he bends over to smell them; cigarette boxes from which frogs jump out; jars of mustard whose lids conceal snakes; fake mice designed to look as real as possible, to be placed in such sensitive spots as kitchen drawers; and many more. The devices are forms of torture aimed at compelling laughter. Woe to him who, on coming across such a trick, says that this is aggression and not humor; he will immediately be accused of having no sense of humor and being unable to take a joke. The boundary line between physical violence and such humor is in fact extremely thin. The balance is very delicate and can be violated at any moment with very unpleasant results. Practical jokes are often degrading and can cause physical injury. An attraction to this sort of humor is without a doubt connected to the innocence and lack of sophistication characteristic of childhood. The "eternal child" in every one of us can express itself with the aid of such pranks. The need to relive something of our childhood days not only exists but receives official recognition on April Fool's Day.

Aggressive humor has indirect forms, too, as in those jokes that work through hints or comparisons:

Mrs X is like the Venus de Milo — she's ancient and knocked to pieces and has yellow stains on her chest.

Finally, the attack may be very sophisticated and still preserve its venom:

Presented here is a list of the banks that place their clients' interests above their own:

All the various forms of aggressive humor can be placed at different points on the graph presented in Figure 1.1. The notice about the banks should go in the lower right-hand section.

I have now tried to show how humor can help us to express the natural aggression in ourselves and to channel it acceptably. Such channels are amusing and socially permissible, and often gain positive credit for the humorous offender. Aggressive humor is an antitaboo device that has undergone a process of socialization. I now proceed to a second taboo that exists in our society — the taboo against sexuality — and examine the ways in which humor copes with it.

2

The Sexual Function
of Humor

APPROACHES TO A SEXUAL THEORY
OF HUMOR

Although sexual humor must have existed since the time of Adam and
Eve, not even one of the dozens of early theories proposed to explain
humor touched upon this type. Freud was the first to emphasize that
one of the important functions of humor was to approach the subject
of sex in a socially acceptable fashion. The truth is that until the coming
of Freud, sex generally was not considered respectable enough to de-
serve scientists' interests. In his great struggle against the objections
of his contemporaries, Freud took sex out of the closet, placed it in
the limelight, and turned it into the concept central to the understanding of personality dynamics. He succeeded so well that, whereas cul-
tured persons during the pre-Freudian period were shocked if someone
spoke about sex, the thought of someone's being shocked when people speak of sex today is what's really shocking.

In Freudian theory, sexuality controls everything human — from
the moral judgment of a child, through the understanding of dreams
and the arts, to the different forms of mental disturbances. Humor,
a very human activity indeed, was integrated into this general outlook
when Freud published his *Jokes and Their Relation to the Unconsciousness*
in 1905.

The main function that Freud attributed to humor — the expression of sexual drive — must be understood against the background of
the period and the dominant world view during his day. The contemporary world view of any theorist most definitely has an influence on
the basics of his theory building.

Let us imagine two geniuses, each of whom could develop a theory that would explain man's behavior. The first of the geniuses takes a walk one bright spring day in Vienna, his birthplace. An arbitrary, almost undetected movement of a certain young woman stepping off the sidewalk happens to catch his eye. While walking, the woman lifts her long skirt slightly above the acceptable height, in such a way that an observer can catch a glimpse of her shapely ankle. Our genius notices that this simple movement causes some rapid changes, both subjective and objective. From a subjective standpoint, he feels a quickening of his heartbeat, a change in his breathing, and saliva collecting in his previously dry mouth. From an objective standpoint, he sees the sparkling eyes of the men currently seated around the tables of a sidewalk cafe. They begin to twist their mustaches nervously as they fix ravenous stares on the "daring" woman. Our genius takes a seat next to a friend at the cafe and says to him, "That woman reminds me of Dreyfus — the army didn't believe his innocence, either." If this genius were to create a theory on man's behavior, we could ask ourselves two questions:

1. What would be the role of sex in this theory?
2. What would be the function of humor in this theory?

Three-quarters of a century later, the second genius arrives at an airport to await his flight to Australia. This is the maiden flight of the world's first plane of its kind: completely automatic. An airplane without a pilot, without a flight crew, even without stewardesses — fully automatic. Our genius makes his way over to the newspaper stand. He takes a bored glance at the stacks of magazines — *Playboy, Playgirl, Playgrandmother,* and the many others like them. Each seems to be competing with the others for the most striking pose or the most original nudity on the front cover.

In a monotonous voice, the loudspeakers are incessantly announcing the arrivals and departures of the various flights in 10 different languages. After buying himself an unusual publication displaying a photograph of one of the latest computers on its cover page and putting on a pair of sunglasses to protect himself from the glaring neon lights, our genius finally gets on the plane.

He sinks into his upholstered seat and listens to the soothing voice re-

sounding from the internal speakers: "Welcome aboard the maiden
flight of the automatic plane. Make yourselves comfortable and forget
your worries. The equipment functions perfectly and any malfunction is
simply impossible — impossible — impossible —."

If this genius were to create a theory on man's behavior, we could, again, ask ourselves the same two questions:

1. What would be the role of sex in this theory?
2. What would be the function of humor in this theory?

The first genius is none other than Sigmund Freud. It goes without saying that it was his theory that enriched psychological science and directed it to areas that, until his appearance, had been ignored. The second genius is a figment of my imagination, and the world is still anticipating his arrival. No doubt he will also arrive, and with him will arrive a theory. Accordingly, there is no doubt that his theory will be less based on the centrality of sex in human behavior. And in its place will be — who knows?

Although the taboo on sexuality has weakened somewhat since Freud's time, the prohibitions surrounding it are still quite strong. Humor enables us to approach the forbidden by hinting at it in a socially acceptable fashion. Sexual humor is exaggeratedly present in situations where acceptable sexual outlets are scarce. In prisons, among sailors spending long months at sea, and even among inhibited teenagers, sexual jokes are more than just frequent. But what happens in general in Western society of the 1980s, in which expressions of sexuality are many, varied, and rather free? Pornographic literature in all its varied forms is permitted and sold without restriction in the Scandanavian countries. "Blue" movies are shown in "specialized" theaters in most Western countries, and publications whose main theme is sex are booming.

Now isn't this a fine satire on Freud's theory? The *logical* conclusion of Freudian theory should have been as follows: As the sexual taboo began more and more to diminish in our society, our need to look for roundabout and hidden means of sexual expression should have gradually weakened and finally disappeared. And is this the case? Not only has sexual humor *not* displayed signs of weakening, and certainly not disappeared, it is alive and kicking!

THE SEXUAL FUNCTION OF HUMOR
IN THE POST-FREUDIAN PERIOD

In a study by Hasset and Houlihan (1979), readers of *Psychology Today* were asked to indicate their preferences from among 30 jokes. Some 14,500 readers responded to the researchers' questionnaire. An analysis of the results indicated that sexual jokes were the most popular. It should be noted that approximately 87% of the respondents had had at least some college education; this would seem to imply that the population had been exposed to all the various media in which sexual topics are expressed freely. It should also be noted that the readers were asked to report the strength of their sex drive. It seems that only 13% of all respondents reported their sex drive as below average. Thus, it can be assumed that this was a "liberated" population in which sexual humor did not fulfill the role that Freud attributed to it. If so, how can we explain the fact that even today, now that sexual taboos have weakened, sexual humor could still enjoy such great popularity in such a group? In my opinion, this question can be answered in two ways. One relates to sexual humor as stemming from the pleasure people find in sex and in the various forms of sexual expression. The second answer stems from disappointment with sex; in this case, sexual humor lashes out at the disappointing aspects of sex. Let us look briefly at these two reasons why humor related to sex is still so popular: the pleasure of sex, and the disappointment in sex.

Humor as an Expression of Sexual Pleasures

Poets have spilled rivers of ink on mountains of paper concerning the unexcelled delights of sex. Personal experience has convinced most of us that the poets are correct. Undoubtedly, sex is one of life's greatest pleasures, which we strive to taste again and again. Alas, our physiological makeup prevents us from unlimited overindulgence. The famous Kinsey report revealed that the average number of weekly orgasms is from two to six (of course, there are age differences). It could well be that we would like more, many more. But there are limits to our physical ability to achieve much more than the average number. Biologists know only one way of increasing sexual ability; this is known as the "Coolidge effect" (see Example 2.1).

    The Coolidge effect, although an effective way of increasing sexual

---

EXAMPLE 2.1
The President and the Bull

While observing a male rat in the presence of a female rat in heat, biologists stumbled upon an interesting phenomenon. When the male is enclosed in a cage alone, he ordinarily runs back and forth, getting to know his surroundings. The introduction into the cage of a female in heat quickly alters the male rat's behavior. He pounces upon her and forces his affections upon her. Immediately afterwards, the rat loses all interest in his female companion and resumes running to and fro, investigating his surroundings. This continues until the researcher decides to remove the female from the cage and replace her with another. Upon the introduction of a new partner, the male's interest is suddenly reawakened. He assails this female and honors *her* with his full sexual attention. Afterwards, the male returns to his previous ways and displays no further interest in the female. When the researcher again exchanges the female rat, the male's sexual interest returns, and so on until the male reaches the point of absolute exhaustion.

Biologists have named this unusual behavior the "Coolidge effect" in memory of a well-known story concerning a president of the United States. President Calvin Coolidge and his wife were visiting a certain farm. In the course of their tour, they came to a field where cows were grazing. A bull had been let into the grazing area. They watched as it mounted first one cow and then a second. When finished with these, it continued on to a third and a fourth. With a gleam in her eye, Mrs. Coolidge turned to her husband and said, "Look what masculine strength!" Coolidge answered, "But look how many partners!" Thus, this American president earned himself a place in biological research.

---

endurance, would probably run into social prohibitions. Despite the sexual permissiveness that characterizes the present age, one cannot simply jump into bed with each potential partner the moment the urge to do so strikes. Social limitations coupled with physiological ones prevent us from achieving sexual satisfaction to the extent we would like. In other words, our appetites are greater than our ability to satiate them.

Sexual humor enriches our sexual experience. Dealing with the subject of sex in the form of humor adds something to help satiate our hearty appetites. Both physical and social limits to the physical satisfaction of sexual needs exist, but sexual humor lets us add to our enjoyment on another level. We can compare the additional enjoyment provided by sexual humor to the French rituals surrounding food and drink. The French are known for their oral passion, which has led to the development of a preoccupation with gastronomy — the art of good eating. A superior cuisine and a complete art surrounding the production of wines are indications of an attempt to satisfy oral needs further. But eating and drinking have physiological limitations. As a result, gastronomy has become one of the main topics of discussion among the French, and a rich, poetic language has developed in order to describe the qualities and tastes of wine. These all increase gastronomical enjoyment without anyone's actually eating or drinking. Similarly, sexual humor provides us with additional sexual satisfaction without our actually taking part in sexual activity.

In psychoanalytic theory, there is a concept known as *sublimation,* which refers to the channeling of drives from their natural spheres into socially acceptable ones. Romantic literature is itself an example of sublimation of the sex drive. Even when the adolescent who displays a precocious interest in sex is told "Go fly a kite!", the meaning of this "advice" is none other than sublimation. However, sexual humor is not to be viewed as real sublimation; that is, it is not a replacement, but rather an addition. Thus, we can see sexual humor in this context as "sublimation-plus." Of course, with all due respect, there is such a thing as sexual enjoyment for its own sake. But because of the limitations that exist, a wide spectrum of additional activities has been created to enrich the experience. Literature, publications, movies, and mere "parlor conversations" are examples of the activities that fulfill the function of "sublimation-plus." Sexual humor falls into this category, as this example indicates:

> *The new ninth-grade teacher approaches her first sex education lesson with some apprehension. She begins: "There are eight basic positions in sexual intercourse — "*
>
> *"Nine!" sounds a voice from the back of the room.*
>
> *The teacher, her timing somewhat disturbed, begins again: "There are eight basic positions in sexual intercourse — "*
>
> *"Nine!" sounds the voice from the back of the room.*
>
> *The teacher decides to ignore the voice this time and continues: "The*

first position is known as the missionary position, in which the man is prostrate above the woman, and they are face to face."

"Aha!" sounds the voice from the back of the room. "In that case, ten!"

Sexual humor contributes to the sexual experience by developing the fantasy element. As I have already mentioned, we are "gifted" with "big eyes" and appetites not always destined for satiation. If we cannot satiate these appetites, at least we can fantasize about what it would be like if we could. Sexual humor can stimulate our sexual desire through fantasy:

One day, when a princess was out walking by the lake's edge, her kerchief fell and vanished into the deep water. After a while, a frog appeared, grasping the kerchief tightly in his mouth. "How can I ever repay you?" asked the princess. "I'm so cold," responded the frog. "Please take me to your bed." And so she did. The next morning, when the princess's mother entered her room and found her daughter in bed with a naked man, she was not at all willing to believe her daughter's story.

Pornographic movies and nude pictures in magazines were created for our stimulation. This stimulation, at least theoretically, should increase our sexual desire. It could be that sexual humor fulfills a similar function: It is used as a "spice" to awaken the appetite. Pornographic literature and the like heighten sexual appetite while trying to compensate for our ordinary physiological limitations. However, from a social standpoint, such "stimulants" have yet to win acceptance. In contrast, sexual humor is capable of helping us in trying to overcome both the physiological and the social limitations that tend to put a damper on our additional enjoyment of sex. Sexual humor not only awakens and stimulates our sexual appetites; it also has the advantage of being socially accepted and even appreciated:

A young woman, all of whose dreams center around one romantic movie star, walks about Hollywood and falls asleep in a park. When she opens her eyes, she sees the hero of her dreams standing across from her.

"You're the prince of my dreams," she tells him.

"In that case," he answers her, "I will grant you three wishes."

"I have only one," she responds, "but you can grant it three times."

In this example, as well as in the preceding one, sex is not even mentioned. The humor lets the listener "assume" sexual elements that are not openly presented. One of the strengths of sexual humor may be that this kind of joke enables the listener's active participation. One must solve a "problem." The listener has to catch the hidden meaning through his own intellectual activity; otherwise, he won't get it. In contrast, nude publications or pornographic movies do not require the active participation of the readers or the audience: The stimulation they afford is direct and simple. Indirect sexual humor, the kind that only hints at sex, contributes to fantasy much more effectively than direct stimuli, at least for some people.

The idea that the hidden stimulates more than the obvious has been very effectively presented by Anatole France (1931) in his story "Penguins' Island." He tells of an island populated by penguins innocently living happy lives in the nude. One day Satan, who apparently has nothing better to do, decides to corrupt the island's inhabitants. Satan obviously must know about the great sorrows fashion can cause, for he decides to take action in just this area. He clothes one of the female penguins, not exactly the most attractive one; in so doing he hides her body, causing the male penguins' imaginations to run wild. The males begin to dream about the hidden treasures that lie beneath the covering. Thenceforth, this female is constantly accompanied by an extensive line of enamored admirers.

So far, in this discussion of sexual humor as a way of adding to sexual enjoyment, I have emphasized the positive side — namely, that sexual humor reflects an attitude of enjoyment, in that it supplements and enriches the experience. However, our attitude toward sex is not always positive. Sometimes sex is disappointing and becomes a source of frustration. These less enjoyable, "biting" aspects of sex can also be found in sexual humor.

Humor as an Expression of Disappointment in Sex

One unexpected result of our liberation from sexual taboos has been the discovery that even sex has its disappointing side. We have all grown up with grandiose expectations regarding sexual pleasure. Our relative sexual liberation now allows us to touch upon the disappointment of these expectations. Freud himself discussed the fact that we are not all convinced of the "pleasance and magnificence" of the sexual experience: "Anyone who subjects himself to serious self examination will indubitably find that at the bottom of his heart he too regards the sexual act as something degrading, which soils and contaminates not only the body" (1912/1959, p. 211).

How did Freud arrive at this conclusion? Since he did not engage in research, it is difficult to know whether this thought is representative of what is found in the minds of most people, but it is a good guess that for at least some, it is. Freud thought that the sexual taboo veils sex in mystery, and that children grow up with the feeling that it is an untouchable subject. That is to say, there is something dangerous about sex — something unpleasant and possibly even damaging. It is difficult to free oneself of such a basic and deeply rooted feeling, even after one is grown up and sexually experienced. However, in the post-Freudian era, sex has been presented in a positive light; as any newspaper stand can prove, it is not at all "veiled in mystery." In fact, it is not "veiled" at all! Still, what happens to a person who is expecting something wonderful, but discovers through his personal experience that sex is not the wonder he was expecting it to be? Surely it is not "fashionable" to talk about the unpleasant aspects of sex, although no doubt they exist, and every adult discovers them at one stage or another. Expectations of supreme experiences, depicted in literature in such lyric phrases as "the earth moved" or "bells rang," are not necessarily fulfilled.

A disappointed person may begin to wonder: Is this state of affairs his own fault? Or maybe his partner is at fault? Maybe both of them? Maybe the myth? It could be that the myth built up around sexuality is based more on dreams than on reality. In reality, sex can be completely different. Sexual intercourse has a clearly apparent biological function, and a less apparent psychological one. The myth claims that the psychological function is to find supreme enjoyment in uniting with the ideal partner. How does this myth compare with reality? See Example 2.2 for a look at some motivations of people indulging in sex.

The reasons listed in the example may be attempts at finding new, interesting, and varied aspects of sex — more than those existing in the widespread romantic myth. If sex can be seen as a means of achiev-

EXAMPLE 2.2
Purposes and Reasons for the Sex Act

In the hope that the present discussion will not cause trauma to those who see in the sex act exclusively "pure" intentions, I present the following list of almost a dozen examples of people's reasons for performing the sex act. These examples are a random sample gathered from interviews with adults.

Physical enjoyment.

Conquest—control and strength.

Ending a fight—reconciliation.

Lessening boredom.

Demonstration of "masculinity" or "femininity."

Rebellion against accepted patterns.

Escape from loneliness.

Curiosity.

Annoyance of or revenge on one's partner.

Overcoming sleeplessness.

Conjugal obligation.

The as yet unshocked reader might have a few reasons of his own to add.

ing such different ends, then it becomes very hard to relate to the myth seriously. When it is difficult to relate to something seriously, the door is opened to humor.

One of the functions of sexual humor is to poke fun at sex and to show its absurdities, as in these jokes:

After making love, the couple is lying in bed. He asks, "Darling, did you ever want to know what it feels like to be a man?"

"No, dear, did you?"

After making love, the couple is lying in bed. He asks, "Did I hurt you?"

"No, dear, why?"

"You moved."

In these two stories — one making fun of a man and the other of a woman, to maintain a balance for sexual equality — the humor relates to the unromantic side of sex. Humor can spotlight the unromantic elements of sex, presenting them in a laughable manner and thus enabling us to look at the disappointing aspects of sex less seriously.

An additional function of sexual humor is to help us cope with the anxieties that the mention of sex is liable to arouse. This aspect of sexual humor is discussed in Chapter 4, which deals with another function of humor — namely, humor as a defense mechanism against anxiety. However, before doing this, I focus in Chapter 3 on another essential aspect of humor: its social function.

3

The Social Function
of Humor

The social function of humor may be considered to have two aspects. The first is that of the relationships *within* a group, and the social system within which personal acquaintance and interaction between and among group members exist. The second is that of society as a whole or of social phenomena, humor's role being to reform aspects of these. Bergson's (1899/1975) theory deals mainly with this "corrective" characteristic of humor. In this chapter, both of these aspects are discussed.

THE SOCIAL FUNCTION OF HUMOR
IN INTERPERSONAL RELATIONSHIPS

Aristotle's remark that man is a social animal has been repeated times without number. From the moment of an individual's entrance into the world, his existence is dependent upon others. The absolute dependence of a baby upon the attitudes and actions of those around him impresses upon him, up until his last day, the necessity of maintaining connections with others. The period of complete dependence is longer for man than for any other animal. The satisfying of the basic needs of existence is a necessary condition for continued life, and by this very agency reciprocal relationships are created between the infant, who at first only demands, and his parents, who initially only give. In the course of a child's development, the process of giving and receiving becomes more and more complex. Parents begin to demand as well as give, and the child gives and does not merely receive. The operation of give and take turns into a process that constitutes a basis for all man's relations with his environment. The medium for this process is communication, and communication's most important tool is language.

The first agreeable piece of "giving" on the baby's part appears well before the development of spoken language, in the smile. This is a form of communication that is welcomed by parents with joy and pride. It is not, of course, the *first* form of communication; a yell is the initial announcement of a baby's arrival in the world. Some cynics hold that it is also the initial expression of opinion about the world, but biologists assert otherwise. And although their explanations are far less amusing or fraught with "philosophy of life," they seem to be correct.

The yell continues to serve as an elementary tool of communication when the message it conveys is "I'm not comfortable." Every anxious mother understands its meaning and hurries to feed or change the child, or to do whatever else will put an end to the vociferous broadcasting of sensation.

In contrast, the smile is the first form of "positive" communication, and it means "I feel good." This message too is readily comprehended by the mother, and it gives her a pleasant feeling. This arises from another aspect of the smile, which she interprets as a sign that the infant recognizes her. The social smile (as against the facial contortions taken as recognition by optimistic mothers) appears between the second and eighth weeks of life and is indeed the first sign of recognition — not of the mother as such, but of human faces and voices in general. Only at the age of about 8 weeks does the selective social smile appear, expressing real recognition. From this age, the baby smiles at his parents and does not smile at strangers.

The message of contentment conveyed by a smile is the basis of laughter. That smiling is the primary manifestation of laughter is also expressed by language, for the word for it in French is *sourire* ("under-laugh"), and in Hebrew it can be called *bat tzhok* ("daughter of laughter").

I may summarize by saying that from the outset, both smiling and laughter carry considerable social weight. They express the satisfaction of the person concerned.

Smiling is a developmental phenomenon whose basis is apparently biological. It certainly appears in all human societies at the same age (Gerwitz, 1965). Later on, at kindergarten age, laughter and smiling are associated with enjoyable experiences, and they accompany the main social activity of children — play. Later still, they turn into physiological expressions of enjoyment, arising principally from humor. As we develop, we become aware that humor leads to laughter and smiling, and that these are signs of enjoyment. The desire to transmit humor is one of the characteristics of man, who is not only a social animal but also a pleasure-seeking one.

Our social development teaches us that the source of the pleasure arising from humor is our fellow man. Humor flowers from interpersonal relationships.

We may approach humor as a process of forming reciprocal relationships that contains three elements: the humorist, the audience, and the subject of humor. Two of these elements may sometimes be found in combination, but in general all three can be separately distinguished. Even when we are alone, absorbed in a book, the author is the humorist, we as readers constitute the audience, and the subject is the particular combination of characters and events described. A man can sometimes laugh when he is on his own, if he recalls something or is a witness to a situation that seems funny to him. As a rule, however, people tend to share humorous experiences together with their friends. Where does this tendency derive from?

Exactly this question was put to Woody Allen in an interview (Lax, 1975, p. 14). He addressed himself to it as a professional humorist who sees his main function as making others laugh. He began with reservations: "What causes a person to go up on stage and tell others stories to make them laugh? It is hard to say." Nevertheless, he tried to tackle the problem and touched on four possible motives. First, exhibitionism and narcissism certainly take a central position. Second, there is the need to form relationships and be accepted. As for the third, Allen said: "Comedians often talk about their wish to see the audience die from laughter"; thus there is apparently an aggressive motive. In conclusion, Allen cited a certain famous Jewish comedian who said, "I have found that people look much better when they are laughing." And from this Allen concluded that the fourth motive is aesthetic — to beautify the human race. No doubt this response should be regarded as an "expert's opinion," but we should not forget that Allen was speaking of the professional humorists' motives.

Fortunately humor is not the sole property of professionals, and I now attempt to delve into the motives behind humor from the perspective of amateurs — that is, most of us. This is done through an analysis of the functions of humor in interpersonal relations from two different points of view. First I discuss the functions that humor fulfills for the individual in the group, and then I touch upon the social functions of humor within groups.

The Social Functions of Humor
for the Individual in a Group

Art Buchwald, the well-known American humorist, has said of his difficult childhood, part of which he spent in an orphanage, "I learned quickly that when I made others laugh, they liked me. This lesson I will never forget" (Buchwald, 1967, p. 15).

Most humorists report the wonderful feeling they get when they make an audience laugh: "The pleasure which I cause them tells me that for at least a short moment, they love me." W. C. Fields said this, but it does not apply only to professional comedians. Apparently we all feel liked when we make others laugh, and we all love people who make us feel good. Humor and the accompanying laughter are important sources of pleasure, as we know from everyday experience, and we like people who are able to cause us pleasure. The great popularity of humorous television shows, comedy movies, or comedy teams proves this in a very convincing way.

Humor can therefore be used as a key for opening up interpersonal relations. A person who wants to be accepted into an existing social group first goes through a stage of "testing." Group members keep looking at him and thinking about him. To some extent, every stranger raises suspicions. Of course, if he wishes to be accepted, he will try to present himself in the most positive light. In this situation, someone with a sense of humor has an undisputed advantage. In bringing laughter to the group, he will win at least momentary affection. The laughter of the group members is a behavioral expression of something shared, and it includes the "new guy" too. If he can laugh at their humor, his chances of being accepted are much greater. On the other hand, if their humor does not in fact amuse him, he may prefer to withdraw and seek other company, and if his humorous attempts leave them apathetic or shocked, his chances of being accepted fall tremendously. However, we are usually aware of the nature of our humorous ability, and we learn by experience whether or not it is a tactic we can use effectively.

To be accepted by and to belong to a group are certainly pleasant. The fact is that we all belong to several groups, even when belonging is not compulsory. This points to one of man's basic needs: the
need for affiliation. Furthermore, belonging by itself is not enough.
It is no less important to win the group's affection, and humor is one
of the many possible ways to do this. But even affection still does not
satisfy most of us. Generally, we also try to obtain status in the group.
One method that children know of is creating social roles. A role that
exists in almost every group is that of "clown." The clown fulfills a number of important functions, and thanks to them he wins a respected
enough position. Among these functions are the following:

1. Creating an atmosphere of enjoyment.
2. Reflecting the views of the group with regard to external factors. For instance, if the clown succeeds in "fooling" the teacher, he
does it to some extent in the name of the class, and the fact that he
dares to do it and they do not wins him appreciation.
3. Absorbing punishment. If the clown is caught after his trick,
he is punished by the teacher; more importantly (for him), however,
he is appreciated by his friends. Because of their identification with
his activity, the other children become partners in the crime. Of
course, they are not active partners, but indirectly their responsibility is expressed in the joint feeling of "fun" that results from the teacher's being made to look ridiculous. The fact that the clown is the only
one who absorbs the teacher's counterblow, while they are not punished, makes him a hero.

These are the means by which the "humorist" child obtains status in
the group. In adolescence and adulthood, the humorous expressions
are more complicated, but they achieve the same ends.

Thus humor can help an individual to climb the ladder of social
hierarchy — to be accepted, to win affection, and to gain status. It can
also help him to avoid sanctions. When a person wants to belong to
a group, he can use humor to investigate its standpoint and spectrum
of opinion without endangering his position. For example, by telling
a not too extreme joke about some political group, he can determine
the group's political climate. Whether the joke triggers waves of laughter or sour faces will indicate on which side he is to stand. And if his
belonging to this group is more important to him than his political

views, he will try to avoid entering into political debates within that framework. Without such a testing of the waters, a serious expression of his political opinions might earn him sanctions on the part of the group, and possibly even rejection.

Another way of avoiding sanctions through the aid of humor originates in the nature of humor itself. Part of the pleasure that is created by every humorous message stems from the awareness that "this is not for real." This awareness offers a respectable way out of expressions or actions that threaten the group. If these were taken seriously, punishment or rejection would follow, but when exactly the same message is conveyed humorously, it is more easily withdrawn. It is enough to say, "But I didn't mean it seriously," and the threat is removed.

The way in which humor prevents sanctions stretches its user's adaptability in social frameworks. Flexibility and adaptive ability are the main components of the individual's assimilation into a group, and the social function of humor is to contribute toward the attainment of this objective. I now go on to the functions of humor within a group.

The Social Functions of Humor in Relations within a Group

In one of his books, Lorenz describes a group of primitive hunters finding their way deep in the forest. Only a few minutes earlier, they have come across a tiger and fought bitterly to kill it. Signs of the encounter are still evident. Their bodies are tense and taut with fear. All of a sudden a rustling is heard. The group is paralyzed with terror. From between the brush a deer dashes forth and darts away lightly. Seeing the frightened deer, the hunters breathe a sigh of relief. The fear melts away and is replaced by a pleasant sense of release, and they burst into laughter. This, in Lorenz's opinion, is the social origin of laughter.

In this example, the laughter stems from the rapid passage from tension to its release. Ever since primitive times, Lorenz (1963) claims, laughter has denoted a situation of security for group members; danger is no longer expected and they can continue their enjoyment together, without suspicion.

In the first anthropological study to be published on the social function of humor in interpersonal relations, Radcliffe-Brown (1940) speaks of what he calls the "joking relationship," which he defines as "a relationship between two people in which one is allowed or even required, according to existing customs, to be ridiculed or to make the other laugh. The other, according to the same customs, is not to be offended by this" (p. 197). In a joking relationship, Radcliffe-Brown sees an example of a peculiar compound of friendship and opposition within the group relationship. In other words, interpersonal humor oils the wheels of communication and permits the establishment of social relations with a minimum of conflict.

The approaches of Lorenz and Radcliffe-Brown both point to one of the main social functions of humor in a group: the lessening of tension and conflicts. These are natural and unavoidable parts of every group's life, but if they continue for a long time they endanger the group's very life and well-being. And just as tension and conflict are causes of division and separation, so humor and shared laughter are factors that join and unite. The experience of shared laughter adds to our feelings of pleasure in the group and increases its attraction.

If we are given a choice between two groups with the same composition and concerns, the only difference being that in one of them there is humor and in the other there is none, there is no doubt that most of us would choose to belong to the first. In the group in which it is possible to laugh, there will be a more pleasant atmosphere, and the other activities and interactions will also be more enjoyable. Furthermore, the conflicts that develop in this group have a better chance of dissolving quickly, which increases the group's cohesion.

Cohesion is one of the main characteristics of groups. A cohesive group is one in which there is a strong attraction between members, which is expressed in a number of external manifestations. In such a group, a member thinks of himself primarily in terms of his membership — that is, the expression "we" is more usual than the expression "I." Members of the unified group spend time together beyond what is required of them. A cohesive group provides its members with defense from external forces. What is humor's contribution to group cohesiveness?

In the model presented by Martineau (1972) for the social functions of humor, he emphasizes the tasks of humor as raising the morale of group members and as strengthening ties between them. He also notes that humor contributes to the maintenance of consensus within the group and narrows the social distances between its members. These tasks of humor receive more importance in stress situations or when members of the group are in crisis. Furthermore, humor also creates a common language. Private jokes are a result of group interaction; these reflect common experiences and cause great pleasure to group members. They create uniqueness for the group because they do not mean a thing to a person from "outside," as this example indicates:

A man sees a group of long-term convicts who seem to be communicating very oddly. One of them says, "7," and they all burst into laughter. Another says "23," and they all explode — and so it continues.

The observer notices that one convict does not laugh at every number, as the others do. "What are they doing?" he asks him.

"They're telling jokes. But because they all know all the jokes by heart, they have given each one a number."

"So why don't you laugh like everyone else?"

"I'm pretty new here. I only know the jokes from 15 to 23."

Private jokes are used, to a certain extent, as a defense against strangers. Because they originate from shared experiences, they strongly emphasize the group's uniqueness and effective superiority over the stranger who does not laugh, because "only the good guys understand." Aggressive humor directed against other groups has the same role. As Chapter 1 points out, this type of humor ridicules and dwarfs others, thus implying the superiority of the group wielding it.

Another aspect of humor's contribution to group cohesiveness is its contribution to social structure. In groups that have a clear hierarchy, humor may both emphasize and blur the hierarchy. These two effects appear to be opposites. However, this is the special adaptability of humor: its capacity to exert influence in two directions and show up the ridiculous in different situations. Its tendency to stress the hierarchical structure was pointed out by Coser (1960), who conducted methodical observations of hospital staff meetings over a period of 3 months. In his lists he noted every "humorous incident" (defined as a comment or story that made most of the participants laugh) that took place. He found that the older staff members directed their humorous comments mostly toward the younger ones. The latter, in comparison, directed theirs toward their hierarchical equals or toward those even lower on the scale — the patients and their families. Similar findings have been reported by other researchers, and my experience as a participant in university staff meetings supports them as well. Indeed, every reader who takes part in meetings can attempt to observe what goes on during them; he can thus learn something about the hierarchy in his organization, and of course can save himself part of the boredom that is inherent in frequent meetings.

When it involves hidden aggression, humor contributes to narrowing the gap in the hierarchical structure. Here, too, much improvization is possible. Consider these examples:

> *The boss turns to an employee who was absent from work the previous day: "Tell me what happened yesterday, but don't forget that your grandmother has already died twice."*

> *The boss says to an employee who arrives late, "I guess my watch is off and needs to be set again."*

Although in both examples the boss holds on to his hierarchical position or even emphasizes his superiority, his approach softens the situation and the hierarchical gap. Comments of this sort, when made jokingly, make both parties laugh and sound less severe than a direct statement. They can certainly be accepted more easily than "I caught you in a lie" or "You're late to work again!" It is important to note that it is not only the content of the comment that is important, but also the tone in which it is made.

Among its various tasks, humor has a part in preserving group norms. In every group, norms originate as to how to behave in certain situations or how to regard certain phenomena. Maintaining and enforcing them is not among the easiest of things, and from time to time one or another group member needs a "reminder." This may be a reprimand or a warning—but not necessarily:

> *Bank tellers as a group have a very clear norm—to take care of the money. One teller describes how he has followed the notices of Bank Lucre:*
>
> *January 15th. Wanted: A head teller for Bank Lucre.*
>
> *February 25th. Mr. Smith appointed as head teller of Bank Lucre.*
>
> *July 25th. Wanted: Mr. Smith.*

Such humorous references to existing norms direct group members' attention toward them and keep the members from ignoring their existence. This way of relating to norms can be much more effective than serious preaching about their importance and about possible punishments for violations. Figure 3.1, for example, presents a sign found hanging in a large planning advisers' office.

Another explanation of the way in which humor preserves group norms arises from Bergson's (1899/1975) theory. Laughter directed at someone who behaves contrary to existing norms is experienced as a kind of punishment, and the offender will take care to mend his ways and avoid further transgressions. In a group of hippies or punks (or whatever fringe group is "in" when this book is read) whose norms include strange clothes and wild hair, a member who shows up with his face clean-shaven, with hair cut and combed, with pants ironed, and with a white shirt and tie on will be brought back to the norms by the laughter of the others, and will very quickly resume the "proper" external appearance. Such norms as dress or external effects, in general, are quite obvious and easily adhered to. But in many cases, norms are by nature more complicated, and their preservation demands more complex measures.

Humor may even be used to execute the norm of justice. Hyghet (1959) tells of an Eskimo tribe in which there are neither written laws nor courts. Justice is carried out in accordance with an ancient custom that tests humorous ability. In a trial in this society, both litigants stand in the center and are surrounded by all the tribesmen. The defendant, who speaks first, attacks his enemy in every possible humorous way, with the sole purpose of getting everyone to laugh. When the plain-

ALWAYS PLAN AHEAD

FIGURE 3.1

tiff's turn arrives, he delivers an address in the same style, with the defendant as the victim. The waves of laughter from those seated round about — who are, in fact, the jury — constitute the decision. The man whose words have evoked a stronger and higher degree of laughter is found innocent, and the man who has demonstrated less talent for making the tribe laugh is found guilty. This method of determining justice may seem primitive to us, but it is not certain that the endless fluent talk and appeals to emotion of a Western lawyer in a 20th-century court are any more logical or any less funny.

There are also social norms concerning laughter itself. Anyone who has served in an army knows the term "short army laugh." Soldiers know that when a superior officer tells a joke, they had better laugh! And, in fact, this is true in any situation in which a hierarchy exists. When someone in a superior position tells a joke or makes a comment that he means to be funny, he expects his underlings to laugh. In such cases laughter is a sign of agreement, for the message transmitted is really "I have a sense of humor, right?", and whoever wants to stay on good terms with his boss had better confirm the boss's assumption, however nonsensical it is. (See Figure 3.2.)

This aspect of laughter as social confirmation exists not only in hierarchies, but among peers as well. If you see a very good cartoon and show it to your best friend, you expect him to respond as you did, by laughing. But if he does not meet your expectations — if he fails to laugh or even to smile — it is as if he were saying, "That's funny? What kind of a sense of humor do you have, anyway?" (this being the friendliest way of expressing the message). If the same thing happens every time you share your humorous experiences with him, a question must arise as to your mutual suitability. Indeed, humor is one of the most important means of checking mutual suitability, and mutual attraction is very often based upon it.

Moreover, let us not forget that the rejection of someone from a group is likely to be carried out by means of humor. The group can turn one of its members into a permanent victim of its wit, thus creating a scapegoat, who fulfills an important task in every group's life. Group members blame him for all their troubles and sorrows, and he is the one who takes responsibility for all their weaknesses and ills. Making him into the victim by the use of humorously biting remarks provides the others with a certain feeling of superiority. Of course the scapegoat can get up and leave the group, but if his belonging to it

FIGURE 3.2

is more important to him than the ridicule and mockery, he will continue to absorb the shock of humor in silence or perhaps even with pride.

The situation is much worse for a scapegoat who has no choice and cannot leave the group at will—for example, an elementary-school pupil. As the scapegoat of his classmates, he is helpless. They can make his life miserable without mercy, and he has no way out. The very worst situation of this sort occurs when a teacher with sadistic tendencies uses sarcastic humor against one of the pupils in his class. The combination of the other children's laughter and the teacher's destructive wit may destroy the child's world.

In summary, it should be noted that all the aspects of group life mentioned here — formation of atmosphere, lessening of tension and narrowing of conflicts, cohesion, hierarchy, and the maintenance of norms — are by no means isolated variables, each standing alone. They are connected with one another and appear in an interlocked and dynamic fashion in every group's life; in its multifacetedness, humor is an important aspect of each one.

Humor has some characteristics that remind one of mercury. It looks like a unified whole until the moment someone touches it. Then it breaks up and scatters into tiny droplets that roll away separately and then draw near again, creating a new united body. Like mercury, humor also has a spark of light within it. It brightens, shines on, and enriches all the factors that compose the dynamics of group life.

Not only small, face-to-face groups are influenced by humor's action. Sometimes humorists try to deal with society as a whole. Ideologies, leaders, accepted ways of behaving, and other "sacred cows" can be laughed at. Laughter, in this perspective, can be seen as a tool of correcting and improving society. Let us now look at this aspect of the social function of humor.

HUMOR AS A SOCIAL CORRECTIVE

Never from its inception has the world been that ideal place in which all man's desires and dreams achieve perfect realization. In consequence, history is strewn with attempts to improve the world and make it a better place to live in — attempts that have taken some very strange and varied forms.

Idealistic notions have arisen in every generation, and they have not always remained merely notions. Some of the most beautiful theories for the advancement of justice, peace, and equality have led, in the process of their implementation, to wars, revolutions, mass murder, inquisitions, and all the rest. All these dreadful things have issued paradoxically from the service of ideals whose ultimate aim has been to create a better world (better, at least, for the relevant group of idealists). The path of action, however, has not always been chosen. People have sometimes contented themselves with preaching, explaining to humanity what constitutes "right" and "wrong" behavior, in the hope that when everyone acts correctly the world too will become good. Not confining themselves to explanation, such preachers have promised rewards to those who do "right" and punishment to those who do "wrong." Such rewards and punishments, moreover, have been guaranteed not to terminate with life, but to continue beyond it. The righteous have been promised a happy life in paradise for all eternity, and the wicked an equal period in the torments of hell.

These attempts to reform humanity by presenting ideals and advancing them by word or action have engaged human beings for hundreds of years, with great seriousness and feelings of self-importance on the part of the presenters. Less serious and self-involved people have held that things might be changed by a less tedious approach — that is, by means of humor. Humor exposes ugly human phenomena (those that render the world almost unbearable) to mockery, in the hope of thereby eliminating them. Man makes a mockery of man. In his efforts at changing and improving mankind, man turns matters he thinks grave into absurdities. He does this sometimes with delicate casualness, sometimes with disrespect, and sometimes with ferocity. The laughter that derives from the perception of absurdity reforms the world. This is the function of humor on which Bergson's (1899/1975) theory principally focuses.

Bergson's theory lays special emphasis on the "educational" function of humor. A human phenomenon that is opposed to society's expectations will meet with punishment, which in this instance means laughter. Thus Bergson writes, "Laughter is a social reaction which punishes and puts down deviant elements in man's behavior and in various events" (1899/1975, p. 76; translation mine). Bergson's theory presupposes that a person or institution that serves as an object of laughter will take care in future not to repeat the behavior that has evoked punishment. Moreover, the fear of becoming a target for mockery should be sufficient to prevent a person from again committing the deed that has led to a punitive reaction. Thus laughter should have the power to change not merely the personal behavior of one individual, but also the behavior of institutions and even whole societies.

Humor of this sort must have a wide scope and must be applicable to the greatest possible number of people. The arts and the various means of mass communication are the means by which humor can fulfill this role.

In the theater, the burden of social correction has traditionally been laid upon comedy. The renowned English playwright Ben Jonson described comedy as an educational instrument: Its goal is not to make us laugh, but to arouse us to moral improvement. The French novelist and critic Stendhal went so far as to set up an "experiment." In *Racine and Shakespeare* (Beyle, 1823), he wrote, "On December 17, 1822, *Tartuffe* was performed. Mdlle. Mars acted well and there was no defect in the play. Nevertheless, the audience laughed no more than twice, and then in a restrained manner" (p. 46). Stendhal came to the conclusion that the aim of comedy is to expose man to the mockery of the audience. People may accept rebuke but cannot bear to be laughed at, and are prepared to be wicked but not ridiculous. The great comedian Charlie Chaplin (1966) has also remarked that the function of comedy is to sharpen our sensitivity to the perversions of justice within the society in which we live.

This "pedagogical" approach seems somewhat overblown to us; if comedy were merely educational, it would be no more effective than a Sunday sermon. Its effectiveness derives precisely from its being humorous. It makes the spectators laugh — that is, it gives them emotional pleasure by throwing the absurd into prominence. Their laughter focuses on the phenomenon that the playwright considers in need of improvement.

Satire, both written and acted, works in a similar way. The satirist is not content with the world as it is; or, more precisely, he is not content with certain things in it, which to him seem black. In his attack he blackens them yet further, in the hope that after blushing with due shame they will turn white.

Comic and satiric theater have the same function — to "reform society" — but there are several important qualitative differences between them. Comedy's criticism of life emphasizes the human side of events and behavior, the good aspects as well as the bad ones. Satire, on the other hand, scourges certain events, sometimes with brutality, and emphasizes their negative aspects almost entirely. As to the preferred topics, comedy focuses on general human characteristics, such as miserliness, hypocrisy, and snobbery. These are to be found in every society, and a humorous presentation of them speaks to everybody. Comedies, therefore, may readily be translated and acted in different countries without losing their relevance. Satire, in general, focuses on situations specific to a given society and period. To understand political satire, the spectator must know something about the political relations and economic background of the society in question. Hence, as a rule (if not always), satire can only rarely be transferred from one society to another. The final difference to be noted here between the two concerns the world views that subsume comedy and satire. Comedy is basically optimistic, and it always has a happy ending. Since it criticizes general phenomena that are fundamentally human and "eternal," the writer of comedy does not expect that the subjects to which he gives a comic treatment will disappear as a consequence of this treatment. He contents himself with showing what is ridiculous about them, in the hope that this will lead to understanding and perhaps a slight movement towards change.

Ephraim Kishon, the Israeli comic playwright and satirist, called his popular column *"Had Gadya"* ("One Only Kid") in allusion to an Israeli song with a structure like "This Is the House That Jack Built," in which each being is in succession attacked by something stronger. Things change, recur, and change once again — or, as the French say, *Plus ça change, plus c'est la même chose.* Writers of comedy are well aware that the subjects with which they deal — infidelity, self-importance, hypochondria, and all the rest — will continue to exist. What comedy really does is to place them beneath a magnifying glass. Exaggeration of the size of each turns it into an absurdity.

In contrast to comedy, satire is fundamentally pessimistic. As I have noted, it deals principally with topical phenomena, and so the satirist expects a rapid change in these phenomena. For example, when political satire attacks a prime minister or a minister of finance (a favorite satiric target), it does so in order to "destroy" the target — in other words, to bring about a resignation. But it is clear to us all, including satirists, that ministerial changes arise from political realities, and that only very rarely does satire succeed in unseating anyone. Here, perhaps, is the mainspring of satire's pessimism: On the one hand, it desires to change actualities, and with dispatch; on the other, it is aware that it is powerless to do so. Moreover, it is almost inevitable that an inability to change matters will be accompanied by a feeling of frustration, which, as we have seen, is one of the main causes of aggression. The element of aggression in satire is certainly far more prominent and embittered than in comedy.

Despite the differences between them that I have noted, comedy and satire possess a common denominator in that both try to change or reform society by means of humor. The two forms together constitute the best illustration there is of the social function of humor.

Comedy is generally received in a friendly spirit. Satire is not. Its victims fear its darts and see it as a threat to their power and position. Thus in totalitarian countries satire directed against the ruling powers is banned, and any manifestation of satire earns harsh punishment. Attacks on a regime through humor must therefore be underground work. Behind the Iron Curtain, there is a most lively industry for humor of this sort:

> *A man who has requested an exit visa to one of the Western countries is summoned to the police station. "Why do you want to leave? Isn't your salary good enough? Is your work too hard?"*
>
> *"No, I can't complain."*
>
> *"Isn't your flat big enough?"*
>
> *"No, I can't complain."*
>
> *"In that case, why do you want to leave?"*
>
> *"Just because I can't complain!"*

In every oppressive regime there is this kind of underground humor, and it fulfills an important function: Laughter shared by the oppressed at the expense of the oppressor reduces fear and helps people to go on living under the regime with more ease. Totalitarian regimes possibly do themselves a disservice in preventing manifestations of humor against themselves, for laughter may be a safety valve for the release of tension and frustration. Similarly, a government that lets its subjects laugh at it evinces its strength, inasmuch as it is not afraid of mockery. Feelings of hostility and frustration may well be increased among the oppressed by the restraint enforced on humorous expression. When such feelings build up and must be held in, a kind of "pressure cooker" is created, which can explode in violent ways. It is to be supposed that in democratic societies, in which freedom of expression is given to political humor, satire indirectly serves the interests of the government. The possibility of ventilating feelings against the state by means of laughter offers release; the hostility might otherwise be demonstrated in far more violent forms, even outright rebellion.

The first piece of methodical research on the function of humor as a mode of facing oppressive social power was carried out by Oberdlik (1942). He investigated the jokes that appeared in Czechoslovakia during World War II, when the country was under Nazi occupation. In analyzing the humor of that period, he stressed its role as a mode of coping with the conquerors. One of his examples is as follows:

> *"Did you hear that the Germans have decided to lengthen the day to 29 hours?"*
>
> *"No, why?"*
>
> *"Because the Führer has promised them that by the spring they'll be in Moscow!"*

Stories of this sort are told when a group or nation finds itself under occupation or oppression without any means of fighting back. In such cases, humor is an instrument of self-respect and the spirit of freedom. The French philosopher Penjon has written, "Laughter is nothing but an expression of the freedom which we experience or long for. Always and everywhere, laughter is the echo of freedom" (1893, p. 113).

I turn now to another aspect of humor: its function as a defense mechanism against life's anxieties.

4

Humor as a Defense Mechanism

In the course of an experiment conducted at the Tel Aviv University, my colleagues and I (Ziv, 1973) invited a group of 4-year-olds to a playroom that contained a sandbox and plenty of toys of all kinds. The children played very happily. At one point we assembled them together and showed them on videotape two 3-minute cartoons, both segments of Walt Disney movies. One featured a pleasant scene of animals meeting in a forest, and the second contained a frightening scene of an ugly, wicked witch concocting a poisonous brew for a fair maiden. After viewing the film clips, the children returned to their toys and played for approximately another quarter of an hour. Before they went home, we told them that they could see just one of the two movies again.

It emerged that the number of children choosing the frightening cartoon was three times greater than the number preferring the other one. Why did the children — of their own free will — choose the frightening stimulus?

We are all aware of the natural tendency to withdraw and escape from frightening situations. Less generally known but no less well established is the fact that the frightening also attracts and stimulates. Stories upon which generations of children in the Western world have been raised — containing such characters as Little Red Riding Hood, who is eaten by the wolf; gentle Snow White, whose stepmother poisons her; and Hansel and Gretel, whom the witch wants to serve up for dinner in her gingerbread house — are only a few of the examples that illustrate the popularity of anxiety among children. And this is true not only of children: Adults also have an undeniable need for anxiety, as is evident from the literature and movies that take advantage of the need for the enjoyment of mankind. Percy Bysshe Shelley's wonderful poetic creations, an inalienable part of world literature, are much less well known than his wife Mary's single publication — a book called *Frankenstein*, which has achieved more translations and publications than all of her husband's great works put together. Frankenstein's monster is one of the universal images that serve as archetypes for creating heightened anxieties. To this group, we can add Mr. Hyde (Dr. Jekyll's alter ego), the Golem of Prague, and many of the heroes of Edgar Allen Poe. Nor is it only literature that provides us with *frissons* of terror. During a trip to an amusement park, haven't you been amazed at the dozens of people lining up, paying good money, and afterwards screaming with fear as they ride the roller coaster?

The creators of this century's most popular amusement, the cinema, discovered man's need of fear very early. An important branch of the film industry is dedicated to the production of frightening movies. People rush to see them; they may become scared or even scream or faint, but in the end they go out satisfied. And generally they go along to the next one. Such movies as *The Exorcist* and *Jaws* have enjoyed exceptional box-office success. In his book on horror films, Peter Haning (1970) reports that Stevenson's story "Dr. Jekyll and Mr. Hyde" has been filmed 13 times since 1908. *Frankenstein* has been filmed 11 times in the past half century. There is no doubt that these movies arouse fear, if only momentarily, in any audience. The moviegoer who chooses this type of film knows what awaits him.

"Thriller" stories, amusement parks, and horror movies are all deliberately set up in order to arouse fear; this is in response to popular demand, without which they could not have become such flourishing industries. As humanity developed, threats to survival lessened. The life of prehistoric man was an incessant fight for survival. He was surrounded by innumerable dangers (beasts of prey and so forth), which forced him to develop nervous and hormonal systems that could be rapidly activated and that heightened his ability to cope with those dangers. The emergence of civilization created comfortable conditions and a system of defenses in which real dangers became quite rare. But changes in the human organism come about much more slowly than environmental changes. As Aldous Huxley (1961) wrote in connection with the reasons for aggression in modern man,

On the physiological level, I suppose that the problem is connected to
the fact that we drag along with us a hormonal system which was suited
to life in the Paleolithic period. But this system doesn't witness good
adaptation to our present lives. We have a tendency to produce adrenalin in amounts beyond what is desired and good for us. (1961, p. 142)

Apparently the organism needs to extract the maximum possible
amount of adrenalin. Since the conditions of life in the modern world
do not provide many occasions for taking full advantage of this potential, man looks about for artificial opportunities. In the routine life
of the average clerk, for example, there are few stormy events that
can give rise to dramatic or dangerous experiences. The lack of agitat-
ing stimuli leads to the search for suspense-creating situations.

Those of us whose need for such suspense is stronger than average
will look for ways of creating genuinely suspenseful situations. This
group (a small minority) consists of mountain climbers, race-car
drivers, skydivers, lion hunters, bull fighters, and the like. Most of
us try to avoid situations in which there is real danger, but suspense
still has great attraction; we therefore seek substitutes, situations in
which there is a pseudodanger that causes tension. The fan of horror
movies seems to go for the purpose of being frightened. But this isn't
so; the truth is that he goes to enjoy himself. And how is it that people enjoy being frightened? The pleasure stems not from the feeling
of suspense, but rather from the "escape from fear."

Fear is accompanied by physiological changes created by surplus
action of the autonomous nervous system, which, as its name implies,
is not voluntary. It is composed of two systems, the sympathetic and
the parasympathetic nervous systems. In situations of fear and anxiety, the functioning of the sympathetic nervous system is dominant.
It causes an increase in heartbeat and in the production of adrenalin.
Blood circulation to the arms and legs increases, in order to prepare
the organism for fight or flight. These physiological phenomena cause
an unpleasant sense of tension. When the fear passes, the parasympathetic nervous system, whose task it is to restore balance to the
organism, comes into action. The lowering of tension is accompanied
by relief. This is an expansive feeling that causes calmness and enjoyment, and to many people it seems a worthwhile compensation for
the moments of tension just experienced.

When we decide to go to the cinema and choose a scary movie, it is clear that we will be frightened, but it is also clear that it won't cause us any actual harm and that in the long run we will enjoy the "escape from fear." When we enter the movie theater, settle into the upholstered seat, and begin to experience the movie's plot with its sophisticated dosage of horror, a situation is created that activates the sympathetic nervous system. If the movie is well made, the sense of fear is so strong that for a moment we forget the fact that we're only watching a movie. Our identification with the victim causes an increased heartbeat, a cold sweat, and all the rest of the symptoms described as characteristic of the fear situation. When the cause of fear in the movie (the monster, the shark, the supernatural creatures, or the mere murderer) is overcome, we feel a tremendous relief. The parasympathetic nervous system takes over, and the organism returns to a state of balance. This is the stage of "escape from fear," which causes us real pleasure.

The relationship between levels of stimulation and pleasure can be explained in the following way: A certain degree of stimulation is pleasurable. Beyond a certain level, the sensitization state causes tension, which becomes unpleasant; we begin to seek ways of freeing ourselves from it. The release from the insufferable tension (i.e., fear) is accompanied by pleasure. Figure 4.1 shows this relationship schematically.

A rise in the stimulation level from low to intermediate produces excitement that is pleasurable (in Figure 4.1, this rise is indicated by the letter A). A further increase to a high level of stimulation is ac-

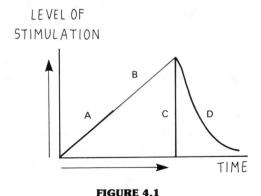

FIGURE 4.1

companied by tension, an unpleasant feeling (B). Any situation leading to a lessening of the tension from the unpleasant level will create a feeling of relaxation, which gives relief. Relief can be sudden (C), but may also be more gradual (D). The main pleasure caused by the release of tension is that which is sought in threatening movies. One of the strange phenomena in a suspense movie is the way in which some members of the audience laugh precisely at the climactic moments. This is probably related to the laughers' inability to deal with the rising tension. They must release their fear, and laughter is the motor and vocal expression of such release.

But how does laughter release tension and anxiety? How can we see an expression of relief in laughter? Several theorists have addressed these questions.

More than a century ago, Spencer proposed a physiological explanation for laughter. His approach is known as the "tension relief" theory: "[L]aughter is the organism's way of freeing accumulated tension" (1860, p. 397). Freud (1905) developed Spencer's idea further and explained laughter as relief resulting from what he called "ideational identification." He illustrated this concept by describing a circus clown's activities. When the clown makes many preparations and after a tremendous takeoff runs at great speed to a jump over a shelf 6 feet up, tension is created in us. We identify with him, and not merely in our minds. We are partners to his preparations, and our bodies are prepared for the jump. But when he reaches the shelf, he stops and goes around it in measured paces. The conceptual and motor tension that has been created in us is released suddenly, and the easiest form of release is laughter.

What happens in anxiety situations? When anxiety is created by observing an unpleasant situation, the disappearance of the situation brings relief, which is expressed in laughter. The higher the anxiety level, the greater the pleasure in its release. This pleasure appears in the form of laughter. An empirical illustration is presented in Example 4.1.

If laughter is one of the physiological expressions of the release of tension and anxiety, humor (which is the principal cause of laughter) can be seen as a way of coping with those phenomena that cause us tension and anxiety. Thus humor fulfills one of its central functions: that of a defense mechanism.

Defense mechanisms are ways in which the individual adapts

EXAMPLE 4.1
Oops! It Wasn't for Real!

An experimenter (Shurcliff, 1968) induced levels of anxiety in three groups of students. He presented each group with the prospect of a different task:

To take a small, quiet white mouse from a box and hold it in their hands for 5 seconds. (This prospect created a low level of anxiety.)

To withdraw a small amount of blood from a white mouse, using a syringe. They were told that this was a simple and easy task. (This prospect created a moderate level of anxiety.)

To withdraw 2 cc of blood from a rat. They were told that it could be expected to bite them through the glove or try to escape. (This prospect created a high level of anxiety.)

When the students approached the cage where the animal was supposed to be, it became apparent that the mouse was a toy. They were asked to evaluate the situation for humor. Their ratings corresponded with the level of anxiety: Those in the group in which a high anxiety level had been induced found the situation to be the most humorous. A correlation was also found between the personal levels of anxiety that the students reported and the humor ratings they gave to the situation.

---

himself to withstand threats. They are subconscious; a person is not aware of his use of them in his behavioral system. At least a dozen concepts have been developed within the framework of psychoanalytic theory to describe types of defense mechanisms. A few of the terms have passed into everyday use and are known to all. One example is the concept of *rationalization* — the "finding of reasons" in order to excuse failures that might threaten one's self-image. We all use rationalization from time to time; the fable told by Aesop about the fox and the grapes exemplifies this idea nicely.

Humor as a defense mechanism has yet to win the attention of psychologists, in spite of the fact that Freud hinted at it in an article published in 1928 under the title "Humor." He wrote,

The principal thing is the intention which humor fulfills, whether it concerns the subject's self or other people. Its meaning is: Look here! This

is all that this seemingly dangerous world amounts to. Child's play —
the very thing to jest about. (1928/1959, p. 220)

In the same article, he gives an example:

> *A criminal being led to the gallows on a Monday observes, "Well this
> is a good beginning to the week."*

That psychological researchers have not grasped Freud's hint is
evident from the fact that the "Humor" article is much less famous than
the book in which he connects humor to aggression and to sex (Freud,
1928). Most researchers have confined themselves to examining humor's aggressive and sexual functions, but humorists themselves are
aware that humor has many dimensions. Charlie Chaplin was aware
of the dimension illuminated by Freud in "Humor"; in his autobiography, he wrote, "A paradoxical thing is that in making comedy, the
tragic is precisely what arouses the funny . . . we have to laugh due
to our helplessness in the face of natural forces and [in order] not to
go crazy" (Chaplin, 1966, p. 327).

In this chapter, I take up the function of humor as a defense
mechanism in two of its characteristic forms, black humor and self-
disparaging humor. I conclude with a connection to one of the topics
I have already discussed — sexual humor.

BLACK HUMOR

> I'm not afraid of death. I just don't want to be there when it happens.
>
> — Woody Allen

> *Little Joey is visiting the zoo with his father. As they are standing by
> the lion's cage, Joey suddenly seems worried.*
>
> *"What's bothering you, Joey?" asks his father.*
>
> *"If the lion gets out of its cage right now and attacks you, what bus do
> I take home?"*

What, in fact is funny in this joke? And what is funny in Figure
4.2? The answer in both cases is that they touch upon one of the

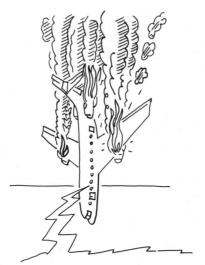

LADIES AND GENTLEMEN, PLEASE
EXTINGUISH YOUR CIGARETTES AND
FASTEN YOUR SEAT BELTS FOR THE
NEXT FEW MINUTES. THANK YOU!

FIGURE 4.2

major human fears: death. The term *black humor* hints at its relation
to the color of mourning. (It would be interesting to know what term
the Japanese use for this type of humor, since in Japan mourning is
symbolized by the color white.) Black humor deals not only with death,
but with subjects that arouse fear in general, as is shown by the inter-
changeable terms for black humor: *horror humor, sick humor, gallows
humor,* and *grim humor.* These nicknames prove that this type of humor
touches upon different situations, all of which have one common
ground—they arouse fear.

The use of black humor enables a person to defend himself from
things that frighten him. Through his laughter at those very things,
he tries to show himself that he isn't afraid. This behavior is like that
of a child walking in the dark at night: In order to conquer the threat
of darkness, he whistles to himself. The whistling's efficacy at driv-
ing away the darkness is identical to that of black humor in remov-
ing the danger of death. Both seem ineffective, but they really are not.

The fact that children use whistling as a defense and adults use black humor proves that these mechanisms do have a purpose, and that they provide a certain encouragement to those who employ them. This comfort stems from one of the most wonderful of man's characteristics — his will to cope and not to suffer passively in the face of the tragedies that threaten his security and his very existence.

The withstanding of dangers can be accomplished through the aid of several defense mechanisms. Resignation is one: "It's my fate — that's how it is — and I have no choice but to reconcile myself to the fact and accept it as the bitter truth." This sort of mechanism involves sadness and depression. Another means of defense is imagining that one can escape the threats: "It doesn't exist; there is no such thing. Maybe it happens to others, but it won't happen to me." In psychoanalytic terms, this mechanism is called *denial*. The result of denial is the construction of an individual world in which a person does away with things that are not pleasant for him. The larger the number of areas that he denies, the greater his distance from ordinary human experience. In addition, he is forced to put out a great deal of energy to repress the anxieties whose existence he is trying to deny. There is also a third defense mechanism, which is to see the dangers, recognize their existence, and attempt to cope with them. This is an "active" way of coping, and it has many forms. Black humor is one of them.

Black humor can be seen as a sort of challenge to frightening phenomena. This challenge carries a number of messages. First, the very naming of the phenomenon indicates that a person has it within his power to face it. Furthermore, not only is he not paralyzed by fear; he even contends that the phenomenon is not really that frightening — and, in fact, that it is rather ridiculous and even funny. His laughter testifies to a sense of victory and control over the situation. The sense of victory as one of the explanations of the phylogenetic development of laughter has been discussed in Chapter 1 in connection with humor's aggressive function.

Piaget speaks of laughter as a reaction to mastery of a situation. In his research on children's games (Piaget, 1951), he notes that the child's first attempts at play to be accompanied by success are acknowledged by a smile. When the child goes on to a more advanced level in the course of his cognitive development, he laughs when he sees other children having difficulty carrying out tasks that he himself was unable to perform at an earlier time. Furthermore, he also laughs when he succeeds at doing something easily that not long ago was difficult for him. Piaget concludes by saying that the sense of mastery is accompanied in the child by satisfaction, which is expressed by smiles and laughter. One of the positive components of black humor consists of a sense of mastery. We are happy to hear of a person who can laugh death in the face, as in this joke:

> Standing in front of the firing squad, the prisoner is asked by the officer in charge if he wants to smoke a last cigarette. "No, thanks," he answers. "I've been trying to give it up."

The laughter (or at least the smile) aroused by this joke expresses our appreciation of courage. We admire the prisoner because he does not take a real threat of death seriously. At the same time, we should not forget that the situation we are laughing at is imaginary: Both the narrator and the listeners are all sitting in a comfortable room, and are not in any danger of death themselves. It is much less certain that we would laugh or react in any way with amusement if we ourselves were facing a firing squad.

But black humor does not only flourish on Saturday nights in the living room. It is often encountered in much less congenial places. Life puts us in situations that would be difficult to endure if it were not for our attempts to lessen the anxiety and the tension associated with them. Perhaps the most outstanding example is war with all its horrors. We may ask what can be funny about war. The answer is people — people who see the absurdity in all those situations in which young people kill one another for the sake of lofty ideals. Have you noticed that most wars are fought for the sake of peace? For the sake of a more righteous world? Isn't this idea itself ridiculous? When we hear one leader or another proclaim in all seriousness, "We export weapons only to those countries that are agents of peace," what should we do? Cry? It's almost certain that crying won't help. Laugh? That won't help either, but at least we'll feel better.

Every year on August 7, a large crowd assembles in Hiroshima, Japan, to remember the victims of the atom bomb. Included in the United States radio broadcast in 1945 was the prayer originally offered for the B-29 plane and the American crew who brought the atom bomb to its target, in which the priest asked God to protect the well-being of the crew members in their task of bringing peace to the earth.

One cannot say that the American priest's blessing arouses laughter. We may doubt whether a person with a sense of humor would have been able to give such a blessing in such a frightful situation. Often, black humor in war deals with this real problem, but in a more delicate way:

> *Before the battle a French soldier tells his comrade, "There's nothing to worry about; we're sure to win. I heard the priest ask God to be on our side."*
>
> *"But the German priest did the same thing," his friend replies.*
>
> *"Really, now! Since when does God understand German?"*

Black humor that succeeds even for a second at turning the horrors of war into something funny helps soldiers to find the smile whose existence they have almost forgotten in the course of fighting. This was the creed of Bill Mauldin (1945), the cartoonist who won a Pulitzer Prize for his work in the American soldiers' newspaper during World War II.

Joseph Heller's exemplary novel, *Catch-22* (1961), also succeeds in dealing with the horrors of war, pointing out its absurdities and thus enabling us to laugh about it. The Korean War won similar treatment in *M*A*S*H*, first as a movie and then as a very successful television series. All this black humor presenting war in a ridiculous light is, in fact, an expression of negation, a rebellion against the phenomenon; it is like shooting an arrow to let the air out of an inflated balloon — in this case, the praises of war from politicians and their kind. This rebellious aspect of black humor supplements its main function as a defense mechanism against the terrible fears of every war.

The humor that flourished in Israel during the Yom Kippur War fulfilled a similar task:

> *Two soldiers are sitting in a small, cramped bar. "You could easily fit an entire tank division in here," says one.*
>
> *"How?"*
>
> *"In an ashtray."*

This sort of humor, which was liable to arouse a shudder among those who had not taken part in battle, achieved great success and reactions of healthy laughter precisely among the tank corps. In the hospitals, also, visitors were startled by the jokes that flew between the soldiers' beds — jokes that the wounded told about themselves or their friends:

> *A soldier who had lost his hand was asked by a friend who came to visit how he had been wounded. He said, "I decided to take the advice of the telephone directory's Yellow Pages — 'Let your fingers do the walking.'"*

This type of black humor, which frightens people who have not experienced the traumatic situation directly, fulfills the function of encouragement for those who have. These individuals encourage themselves with the aid of a nonserious approach to very serious matters, which neutralizes the horror and even makes it possible to rise above it. In this way, they also encourage their friends by showing them that, in spite of disaster, it is still possible to smile and even to laugh. In this aspect of self-encouragement, there is a sort of provision of strength for coping with the tragic situation. The bitter reality cannot be altered; what can be altered is one's attitude toward it.

Different ways of perceiving reality lead to different modes of behavior. The perception of a traumatic situation accompanied by helplessness can lead to the creation of an unrealistic world in which one's identity is lost. In schizophrenia, for example, the person makes for himself a world that only he can understand, and so cuts himself off not only from reality but also from the general population surrounding him. Black humor also relates to the traumatic situation through fantasy. However, this fantasy does not attempt to cancel out reality; rather, it aspires to cope with it through distortion of its shape. Despite the courage of such attempts to cope, there is a sad element in black humor. Usually it arouses no real laughter, but only a smile (occasionally bitter), for the pleasure we have in it is combined with distress.

In an article entitled "The Nature of Laughter," McDougall (1903), a well-known American psychologist, wrote that humor is not an expression of pleasure. Situations that give rise to laughter are in fact unpleasant, and if we do not laugh at them, they will cause us suffering. Laughter is nothing but an immunization that nature kindly provides for us against feelings of overidentification and sympathy. The development of society forced man to improve his ability to understand his fellow man. Thus the ability to sympathize developed — the source of prosocial behaviors of altruism and mutual help. Overdevelopment of the ability to sympathize, however, could cause tremendous suffering; to understand this, one only has to think of the thousands of things that bring sorrow and pain to others. In order to live with this potential for suffering, man has had to create a system of defense against identification. Instead of identifying with his and others' daily sufferings, he laughs at them.

Bergson also touched on this aspect of humor: "In order that humor be effective there must be a momentary emotional dimness of heart, and a turning to the intellect" (1899, p. 9; translation mine). Mark Twain once said that the hidden source of humor is not in happiness, but in sadness: "There is no humor in the Garden of Eden" (Clemens, 1935, p. 185). Where everything is perfect, there are no tensions, no reason for dissatisfaction, no grounds for criticism or fear — and therefore there is no place at all for humor, particularly black humor.

So far, death and war and its results have been mentioned as the main subjects of black humor. But the list of reasons for fear and anxiety does not end with these. The world in which we live seems to be rational, but occasionally we encounter phenomena that cannot be explained. The popularity of astrology, parapsychology, and science fiction indicates our attempts to understand phenomena over which we have no control and that we do not understand. Superstitions were created by the efforts of primitive man to understand mysterious natural phenomena. Modern man places his full belief in science, which would seem to absolve him effectively from the need to understand. When he presses a button, as if to say, "Let there be light," it is taken for granted that there will be light. When he presses another button and watches an event taking place at a distance thousands of miles from where he is seated, there is no wonder in this. And even when he is seated in a plane and the pilot reports, "We are flying at an altitude of 30,000 feet," modern man doesn't even bat an eyelash. But the man who accepts these technological miracles as natural phenomena without actually understanding anything about their functioning will shudder at the sight of a black cat crossing his path, will take care not to walk under a ladder, and will cross his fingers until his supersonic jet lands safely. When this modern man wants to know what the future holds for him, he will snatch a glance at his horoscope and then either relax or put off his business until he gets further directions from the next horoscope. His belief in science is not as firm as he tries to make it seem. His primitive suspicions have not died, and they continue to gnaw at his heart, side by side with his faith in science, order, and logic.

This coexistence of the rational and the irrational is fundamental to human nature. One good illustration of this can be found in New York, a city whose skyscrapers and hyperadvanced technology are symbols of rationality and scientific progress. But, when ascending in the elevator of any skyscraper in the city, one encounters a very irrational phenomenon: Mathematics, the most exact of the sciences, gets a resounding slap in the face from all the elevator manufacturers and from the people who use elevators. The orderliness of numeration is shattered when, in contradiction to all rational thought, the 14th floor comes after the 12th floor. The irrational fear of the mysterious number 13 is alive and well and living in New York. Change is the essence of every science; yesterday's theories and proven facts appear ridiculous today. In contrast, superstitions do not suffer from the upheavals and instability that characterize scientific thought. They are a part of humanity's collective subconscious, and no scientific advancement can change that.

The fears of the collective subconscious are taken care of by black humor, too:

> *A little girl, very frightened in the dark, asks an older man passing by: "Sir, could you please help me and walk with me through the cemetery? My home is on the other side."*
>
> *"Sure," says the man, and he walks hand in hand with the girl through the tombs.*
>
> *"Thank you, sir," she says. "I am really afraid to walk in the cemetery during the night. Aren't you afraid?"*
>
> *"Not now, my little girl, but when I was alive I wouldn't have dared pass through here at night."*

Charles Addams's famous cartoon series places a most unrealistic family in rational situations, which they then have trouble dealing with. The mother looks like a witch, elegant but dangerous; the father is a figure of horror whom it would be better not to meet on a dark night;

the children are sadistic little monsters; and the servant is a perfect double of Dr. Frankenstein's creation. This charming family has succeeded in amusing millions of readers, precisely because of its supernatural image and its inability to adjust to the real world.

In the cinema, Mel Brooks's movie *Young Frankenstein* achieved tremendous success, as did Roman Polanski's movie *The Ball of Vampires*. The directors of these films and many other artists are successful because they help us to encounter irrational and frightening images and situations and to turn them into funny ones. The opportunity that we are given to laugh at things that are basically frightening or sad protects our mental health. Black humor is an active defense mechanism that helps us to cope with threats and fears instead of surrendering to them. For this reason, perhaps, Mishkinsky (1977) suggests that humor should be thought of not as a defense mechanism but as a "courage mechanism." If we called black humor a "courageous defense mechanism," this could emphasize its importance. Turning the frightening reality into fantasy, or the frightening fantasy into the ridiculous, is in brief the essence and strength of black humor.

As I mention at the beginning of this chapter, black humor is only one form of humor as a defense mechanism. Another form is self-disparaging humor, which I now consider.

SELF-DISPARAGING HUMOR

Look how strong I am, I can even show that I'm weak.

—L. Weiss

In Chapter 1, I mention ethnic humor briefly. The purpose of this type of humor is to hold a certain ethnic group up to ridicule, and in this way to feel superior to it. An old Jewish joke begins by making fun of the "oppressor" ethnic group in Tsarist Russia at all its levels:

If you tell a joke to a Russian farmer, he'll laugh three times: once when you tell the joke, the second time when you explain it to him, and the third time when he finally understands it. But if you tell a joke to a Russian landowner, he'll laugh twice: once when you tell it, and once when you explain it. Understand? He'll never understand. If you tell a joke to a Cossack, he'll only laugh once: when you tell it. He won't let you explain it, and he certainly won't understand it.

And if you tell a joke to another Jew, he won't laugh at all. Before you finish the story, he'll stop you and shout, "I've already heard it! Besides, I tell it a lot better than you do!"

In contrast to most ethnic humor, in which the victim of the laughter belongs to another group, this story has a small addition in which the narrator's own group is also presented as no less absurd than the others.

What is the psychological meaning of humor in which a person makes himself or his group the victim? Is this intellectual masochism, as in Bergler's opinion (1956), or is it the opposite? That is, is the ability to present one's own weakness actually a declaration of strength, as the philosopher Weiss (1952) contends? Both explanations are correct to some extent, and it is possible to add a third. Maybe the best way to understand self-disparaging humor is to take a look at Jewish Diaspora humor. I should like to emphasize *Diaspora* humor, since this form of humor is not so characteristic of Jews in the Holy Land. Mindess (1972) discusses the difference between Jewish humor in the Diaspora and in Israel and emphasizes some characteristic images in Jewish humor in general: the *schlemiel* and the *chutzpadik*.

Diaspora Jews have remained in love with the *schlemiel*, the clumsy figure who is always getting into difficulties; therefore, the talent for self-ridicule is an outstanding feature of their humor. Israelis, for various reasons (some clear and others not), identify mainly with the *chutzpan*, a person of nerve and impertinence. Israeli humor is mainly of an aggressive sort whose preferred form is satire. When it laughs at Jews, these are "other Jews" who belong to the wrong group: to another political party, another community, and so on. Of course, this is not to say that self-ridicule is completely absent from the Israeli scene, for it isn't easy to get rid once and for all of the Yiddish folktale heritage of wise idiocy that Israelis drag after them to this very day. Israelis, like others, are able to laugh at themselves and their way of life, as in this instance:

Typical advice of an Israeli to a person interested in immigrating to Israel: "Do you want to have a small fortune in Israel? Very simple: Bring a large fortune with you."

But, as mentioned, this sort of humor doesn't really characterize Israeli humor; it is more typical of the Diaspora.

For many generations, Jewish life in the Diaspora was one long chain of threats, dangers, and disturbances. The Jews developed a bitter humor against their oppressors' attacks, in which they put themselves down. Freud wrote, "I don't know if there is another example of a people who knows how to make fun of its own character like the Jews" (1905/1916, p. 157).

Reik (1954) notes that the special character of Jewish humor is that its source is in the opposite of its self-perception. On the one hand, the Jews of the Diaspora saw themselves as a "chosen people"; on the other, they lived under conditions that put them at the bottom of the social ladder. So they took themselves both seriously, as people who provided a great model to others, and unseriously, as people who saw their weaknesses and inferiority and could live with them. Self-disparaging humor may be used as a defense mechanism against those very weaknesses. It is as if they were saying, "What's so bad about them? I can laugh at them." Consider this example:

> *Three Jews who have been sentenced to death are standing in front of the firing squad. The officer asks the first one, "Do you want a blindfold?"*
>
> *"Yes," answers the Jew, and he is given one.*
>
> *The officer turns to the second: "Do you want a blindfold?"*
>
> *"Yes," he answers, and he is given one.*
>
> *When the officer addresses the third with the same question, he replies, "No, I don't."*
>
> *The second Jew leans over and whispers to him, "Moishe, stop making trouble."*

One message of self-disparaging humor to the enemy could be run something like this: "You don't have to attack me and damage my honor — I'll do it myself (and even better than you)!" In addition, the enemy's laugh may discharge his hostility, so that he does not use his weapon. It is better to look scared, miserly, and foolish, and to stay alive, than it is to die.

Self-disparaging humor is not just a defense mechanism for a peo-

ple as a whole, and it certainly is not the exclusive property of Jews.
It is found among other peoples and fulfills the function of defense
mechanism for them as well. It functions as a defense mechanism on
the individual level, too. When Edmond Rostand looked into the mir-
ror on his 75th birthday and said, "Mirrors aren't what they used to
be," he personified the individual aspect of self-disparaging humor.
The same can be said about Abraham Lincoln, who, in response to
an opponent's accusation that he was two-faced, said, "I leave it to you:
If I had two faces, would I use this one?"

An interesting psychological phenomenon is that a person's ability
to laugh at himself is thought of as a desirable trait and wins appreciation. When my colleagues and I asked students if they used this type
of humor, almost all of them answered in the affirmative. When asked
to give an example from personal experience, they were dumbfounded;
they stiffened and kept silent. Why does man's ability to laugh at
himself have such a high social desirability? Maybe just because it *is*
so rare? People take themselves very seriously and put a great deal
of effort into presenting themselves in as positive a light as possible
in front of others. Because of this, they suspect that presenting themselves humorously will hurt their image.

If we listen to a person describing something that happened to
him with someone else, we hear a conversation that generally goes
something like this: "He said . . . *and then I* said . . . and he said . . .
and so I told him . . . he also tried to say . . . *and so* finally *I* told
him. . . ." The simplest analysis of the content of this story will quickly
uncover the fact that the wise and logical remarks generally follow "then
I said . . . ," while the other person's statements are vacuous and un-
convincing. The moral of the story is this: "See how smart and witty
I [the teller] am; see what a strong character I have."

No matter how funny this may sound, it is far from rare. It reflects the person's desire to project a positive image. We often describe
certain characteristics positively when they relate to ourselves and
negatively when they apply to others. The average person's articles of
faith can be summarized with the help of a list like this one:

I	*You*
I am consistent	You are stubborn
I am flexible	You give in
I am cautious	You are a coward

Despite our attempts at presenting ourselves in a positive light, all (or at least most) of us are aware of the fact that we are not perfect. The stubbornness, the giving way, and the cowardliness that we so easily ascribe to others are our inheritance, too. But the fear of damaging our positive image makes us do whatever we can to hide our negative aspects.

What person can dare present his weaknesses without fear of rejection? Who is the one who can see and show his absurdities? And how is this sort of person seen by others? Let us consider both persons involved in the process of self-disparaging humor: its user and his listener.

The user of self-disparaging humor apparently has one central psychological characteristic: He knows and accepts himself with all his complexities. He is aware of the positive and strong aspects of his personality, as well as of his weaknesses and absurdities. He is open enough toward himself to comprehend all his various characteristics. It's safe to assume that he is an introvert who invests a great deal of self-understanding — more so than the extrovert, who is mainly occupied with understanding those surrounding him and their reactions toward himself.

The user of self-disparaging humor demonstrates self-insight as well as high self-acceptance. What is his incentive for publicly presenting his weaknesses? Most of us, even if we know our weaknesses, don't go waving them around for all to see. It seems to me that there are three main purposes for a person's use of self-disparaging humor, and that all three are forms of defense mechanisms. The first motive is to deter aggressiveness. If a person can laugh at his own weaknesses, he prevents others from laughing at them. By presenting his negative characteristics, he removes the others' potential weapons and doesn't allow them the chance to attack him. One pleasure to be derived from humorous assaults is that of viewing a person's weaknesses through a magnifying glass. When a person does that himself and emphasizes a particular weakness, the motive for an attack on it disintegrates.

Among comedians, there are some who make a fortune from stressing their psychological and physical weaknesses. Joanne Merill, for example, is a delightful comedienne who weighs about 260 pounds. In one of her routines, she says, "I don't want to add to the comments on my body structure, but there are those who say that if I was in India I would be holy." In the audience's laughter, there is both an element of appreciation (at her courage for laughing at herself) and the loss of any further desire to laugh at her rotund shape.

Another well-known American comedian, the late Jack Benny, used his stinginess as a main subject. At every opportunity he emphasized this trait, and it certainly did not occur to anyone to attack him for being stingy.

This purpose of self-disparaging humor recalls what we've already said about Jewish humor: "Don't attack me — I'll do it myself (and a lot better than you could)!" But the power of self-disparaging humor against aggression is not simply that it deters aggressive motives; it is also likely to arouse a wish to help and encourage the person who has uncovered his weaknesses. When I discussed this topic with students in a seminar on the psychology of humor, one of the students told how he had used self-disparaging humor as a sort of technique for picking up girls. During their first encounter, he would confess that he was rather clumsy and didn't really know how to act around girls. As a result, some girls felt almost obliged to help him in the area in which he had admitted inadequacy.

A second motive for using self-disparaging humor is to achieve appreciation. The person concerned knows that the personal trait being ridiculed is present in others to some extent, too, and his self-disparagement enables them to identify with him. This is a "safe" identification, because someone identifying with the weakness does not actually say that he is like that too. The self-disparaging humorist allows such a listener to see that another person also has this trait, and not only dares to talk about it but can even laugh about it. This identification can win sympathy, appreciation, and even love for the person who dares to touch and laugh at the weakness that exists in us, too.

The third motive for self-disparaging humor is to enable a person to grapple actively with the fear that his weaknesses arouse in him. A person who can talk and laugh about his inability to make decisions, difficulty in expressing himself in public, or any other problem is likely to be encouraging by the very fact that he can present these weaknesses for show and can laugh at them. It is as if he were saying to himself (and to others), "If this demon is funny, it's a sign that it's not so terrible." This is an attempt at minimizing weaknesses. If the person could not laugh at them, the awareness of them might lead to anxiety, self-pity, or even the need for long-term emotional help.

In discussing these three purposes of self-disparaging humor, we should not forget that in addition to being a defense against anxiety, this humor can fulfill other functions — in particular, the emphasizing of superiority. A person who is sure of his social position, especially in terms of the hierarchical structure, is likely to use self-disparaging humor in order to show others that he is able to relate to his weaknesses lightly. This can give the (sometimes totally incorrect) impression that this is his only real weakness. This aspect of the use of self-disparaging humor belongs more to expressions of superiority and less to defense mechanisms; however, generally, the main function of self-disparaging humor is defensive.

What process does the person who listens to self-disparaging humor undergo? I have already pointed out most of the psychological phenomena involved. He admires the other person's ability to laugh at his own weaknesses. He identifies with the other, since those weaknesses are often present within himself too. Likewise, being a witness to self-aggression constitutes partnership in an aggressive act; as Chapter 1 indicates, participation in such an act lessens tension. The lessening of tension is accompanied by pleasure.

However, there is an additional aspect that has not yet been mentioned — that is, an addition to the *listener's* feeling of superiority. The moment someone declares his weaknesses in public, others can have a feeling of comparative superiority, which, being pleasurable, is expressed in a smile or laughter. It may seem that this sense of superiority contradicts the feeling of identification with the person laughing at himself; this is correct. People are made in such a way that they can enjoy something and its opposite at the same time. The pleasure that stems from superiority does not lessen the pleasure that stems from identification.

What black humor and self-disparaging humor have in common is the preservation of self-image and emotional balance. Humor is used as a defense mechanism in any situation that poses a threat to these factors. The number of horror jokes heard in hospitals and operating rooms would shock any healthy person. But for doctors who are busy day in and day out with human tragedies, humor provides a sort of counterweight that enables them to preserve their emotional balance. It sometimes prevents the decline into depression that is natural under the circumstances in which doctors work.

The topics that might arouse anxiety in us are almost innumerable. One subject that is not usually considered to have connotations of anxiety is that of relations between the sexes. I have already discussed these relations and their more and less positive aspects in Chapter 2; I hint there that sex as a subject arouses anxieties in us. Humor can fulfill a defensive function in the presence of this kind of anxiety.

HUMOR AS A DEFENSE MECHANISM AGAINST SEXUAL ANXIETIES

Sexual humor functions as a regulator of our thoughts on the subject of sexual intercourse. By the term *regulator*, I mean a force that contributes to a normative organization of the system of sexual relations. Humor that ridicules "unacceptable" forms of sexual intercourse acts as such a normative force. Sexual humor enables us to approach subjects in the area of sex that arouse anxiety: homosexuality, frigidity, sexual indifference, impotence, and so on.

Mention of these subjects is apparently deeply embedded with taboos, even more so than general sexual subjects. And once again, humor allows us to approach these subjects without anxiety — or, at least, with less anxiety. By making the frightening elements of sexuality seem ridiculous, the intensity of the anxiety aroused is lessened. Likewise, the humorous expression of these subjects fulfills a release function. There are three regulating elements:

1. Touching upon anxieties connected with sex.
2. Presenting them in a ridiculous light.
3. Producing relief from the influence of anxiety.

These elements are connected to one another in such a way that one makes possible the passage to the next. The relationship among them is described schematically in Figure 4.3. Approaching these subjects arouses anxiety; however, the moment humor enters, the level of anxiety is lessened. Changing the frightening into the ludicrous causes laughter, which indicates release. This release lessens the strength of the fear and leads to renewed approaches toward these sensitive subjects. This circle exemplifies the contribution of humor to coping with anxiety-arousing subjects, of which sex is only one.

On the one hand, sex is a primary source of pleasure and joy, and on the other hand, it gives rise to much concern and anxiety. Fan-

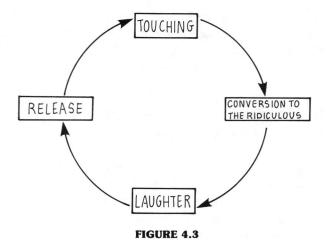

FIGURE 4.3

tasies and anxieties related to sex are definitely individual matters; certain ones, however, are common to us all. Undoubtedly one of the main sources of anxiety is impotence in men and frigidity in women.

> *A young woman says to her therapist, "Doctor, is this normal? Every time my husband and I have intercourse, I feel either very cold or very hot."*
>
> *After a series of tests in which no cause is discovered, the doctor calls in the husband and asks his opinion about the phenomenon his wife has reported.*
>
> *"It's quite simple," says the husband. "Once in the summer, once in the winter."*

This humorous attitude is rather pessimistic, but the same problem can be approached in a more optimistic spirit. A different joke touches upon another source of anxiety as well — sex in old age:

> *An old woman goes to see a psychiatrist. "Doctor, my husband worries me. I'm afraid he's losing his potency. I'd like to know if the reasons are physical or emotional."*
>
> *The psychiatrist, a bit surprised, thinks a moment and asks "Could you tell me your age, please?"*

"I'm 80," the woman answers.

The doctor considers again, smiles suddenly, and asks, "And what is your husband's age?"

"He's 85."

This time the doctor looks perplexed. "Madam, when did you first discover that he was impotent?"

"The first time was yesterday evening. But what really worries me is that it happened again this morning."

In both these stories, the victims are of both sexes; however, in most sexual jokes, the woman is the victim of the humor. There are many reasons for this, including two that seem particularly important. The first stems from the fact that most creators of jokes are men. In Western society, vulgarities are more acceptable among men, and the prevailing explanation is that women are "too gentle" to deal with these indelicate subjects.

The second reason touches upon men's need to create this kind of humor. I am of the opinion that the amount of antifeminine hostility in a considerable portion of sexual humor is based on man's biological weaknesses (see Example 4.2). Fry (1972) suggests that men's biological inferiority has had an important influence on the sexual humor that they create and enjoy. Sexual jokes told to or by men reflect their inferiority in relation to women. In addition, it could be that the myth of the aggressive and dominant strong man is nothing more than a form of compensation for biological inferiority, and part of man's struggle to present himself as stronger than woman. In this way, men's sexual humor about women fulfills the function of a defense mechanism against their environmental anxiety in the presence of the sex that is truly stronger.

Subjects normally regarded as sexual problems often relate to normal everyday phenomena. Lack of masculine strength, frigidity, and aging are subjects that touch all men and women at one point or another in their lives. This may be another factor in the enjoyment of sexual humor. We are anxious about these "normal" phenomena, and presenting them in a funny light may lessen the strength of their threat and scariness.

Humor's regulation of sexual areas that arouse anxiety also covers

EXAMPLE 4.2
The Strong-Weak Sex

Members of one sex are stronger than those of the other; this is a known fact. However, the one generally called the stronger has too many biological weaknesses for the prevailing myth to be taken seriously.

Research has systematically produced a chain of data regarding sex differences that favors women. Despite the facts that at birth male babies weigh more and are noisier than females, and that as adults men have larger hearts, larger stomachs, and longer limbs (which enable them to run faster, jump higher, and lift heavier weights), men have many more biological weaknesses than women. Large numbers of physical defects are almost completely confined to males. Hemophilia, mitral stenosis (a type of heart defect), congenital deafness, color blindness, and baldness—all these are practically the sole property of the "stronger sex." The percentage of male premature infants is higher than that of females (the ratio is 140 to 100). Birth accidents that result in death occur among males 54% more frequently than among females. In the first year of life, 56% of incidents of death are among males. At the age of 21, the percentage is 68%, and at age 35, it is 58%.

The life expectancy of women is higher than that of men. There are those who attribute the higher death rate among men to the social function they fulfill; such theorists contend that men are more often exposed to different types of stress, and therefore die younger. However, a famous study conducted in the United States (Oakley, 1972) destroyed this notion. It compared the life expectancy of 30,000 Catholic nuns to that of 10,000 Catholic monks. Both groups live in more or less similar conditions: They are all unmarried, are often teachers by profession, do not smoke or drink, follow the same discipline, are quite healthy generally, and receive identical medical treatment. The results showed that in this population the life expectancy of the nun was significantly higher.

aspects of sexual behavior that are further from most people's everyday experience—homosexuality, for instance. Many jokes are told about homosexuals, their dress, and their behavior. This laughter, in Freud's opinion, is a frightened response to a deep anxiety within all of us, because we are all bisexual beings. Not only do we go through a homosexual phase during our sexual development, but the latent tendency remains with us throughout our entire lives and causes us to fear anything connected with homosexuality. This is apparently the basis for popular humor directed against homosexuals. In this connection, one of Woody Allen's jokes is appropriate:

I'm a heterosexual, but there are advantages in bisexuality. It doubles your chances for a date on Saturday night.

In the past few years, increasing permissiveness has enabled us to touch more freely (at least intellectually) upon the complexities of heterosexual and homosexual relations, as in this joke:

A gay couple is watching the passers-by. A pretty girl goes by, swinging her hips; her tight blouse emphasizes her curves. Following her with his eyes, one of the homosexuals says to his friend, "You know, sometimes I'm sorry I'm not a lesbian."

Coping through humor with the anxieties that stem from relations between (or within) the sexes adds an additional dimension to all that has been presented in this chapter. There are many things in life that threaten us and arouse anxieties in us. The mature personality is acquainted with this aspect of life and grapples with it in many different ways. Humor has a very important task in this war with the many difficulties of life. Thus it fulfills one of its main functions: as a defense mechanism in the presence of anxiety.

I now examine a rather different function of humor — it's intellectual one.

5

The Intellectual Function
of Humor

Enjoyment of humor in all its modes depends on one necessary condition: understanding the message. (It is necessary, but not sufficient; later on, I discuss the other conditions required for the enjoyment of humor.) I have said "necessary," because if a person does not understand a joke, there is no chance of his enjoying it. Understanding is a part of the thought process, and the enjoyment of humor calls for an intellectual activity like the kind required in problem solving. The need for intellectual activity is even more pronounced where creating humor is involved. The originator of humor must present his message in a certain way, and this demands some planning.

The intellectual activity that accompanies the production and enjoyment of humor represents the intellectual function of humor. Intellectual activity that leads to understanding causes enjoyment and satisfaction. The source of satisfaction is the conscious proof of our ability. Often when we are trying to deal with some problem, and then find the solution, we are filled with a good feeling. This feeling is not infrequently accompanied by a smile, or even an outburst of the laughter of success. Every intellectual success bring about a better understanding of one's surroundings, which, among other things, provides a sense of mastery over the environment. In order to understand how this mastery (which is pleasurable in itself) develops, let us review briefly how a child learns to enjoy humor.

In Chapter 3, in connection with the social function of humor, I discuss the meaning of a baby's smile. After the smile becomes meaningful—that is, after it has begun to represent recognition of an image—it appears when the child is presented with new stimuli. A stimulus that is completely new and not at all similar to anything the child has seen before causes curiosity and an attempt at manipulation. This is the child's effort to understand and master his environment. If the stimulus is to a certain extent similar to stimuli with which he is already familiar, his curiosity will be accompanied by a smile. That is, the effort he must exert in order to place the new stimulus in his world is not too great, but it is still an effort. Kagan (1971) notes from his research that the smile appears in the child as a reaction to a stimulus that requires an "optimal effort" to be recognized. This does not mean a great effort, which would probably render the child unable to place the stimulus in his world. In such a case, the new stimulus is likely to cause a reaction of disquiet and fear. But if a new stimulus is presented before the child time after time, then after a certain period a smile will appear. This smile is a translation of his adjustment to and acquaintance with that stimulus. If the presentation is still continued, however, the smile disappears. Overadjustment causes boredom, and apparently babies do not like to be bored any more than adults do.

This phenomenon is paralleled in research on the problem-solving process in children (Harter, 1974). When children are given a problem, such as sketching a way out of a maze or putting a picture together from pieces, it has been found that they smile as they arrive at the solution. The more complicated the problem being solved, the broader the smile. Of course, if the problem is too difficult and the child does not manage to solve it, there is no smile. Hence there is a connection between the problem's level of difficulty and the amount of enjoyment involved in finding its solution. The smile is an expression of this enjoyment.

Thus we can see that children, as well as adults, enjoy activating their intellectual processes. Through them, they achieve a better knowledge of their environment and gradually attain mastery of it. Furthermore, every intellectual activity that ends in success — for example, the finding of a problem's solution — produces a sense of victory. And, as Chapter 1 indicates in regard to the aggressive function of humor, a sense of victory causes enjoyment.

In the development of laughter, we find a similar phenomenon. The laugh appears at the age of approximately 4 months and is connected mainly with tickling. At the age of 8 months, it can be aroused by a game in which one hides behind something and then uncovers one's face ("peek-a-boo"). At the age of 1 year, unsuitable behavior on the part of the mother (such as drinking from the child's bottle or walking on all fours) causes laughter, in one of the first indications of amusement founded on incongruity. Incongruity is the basis for understanding the intellectual aspects of humor. It creates some kind of problem, and our curiosity, combined with a desire to activate our intellectual ability, encourages thought. It follows that it is possible to see in a situation of incongruity (which is at the base of all humor) an opportunity for problem solving. This is undoubtedly a mode of intellectual activity, and it is activated in every understanding of a humorous message. But as I indicate later on, despite the similarity between the intellectual activities of problem solving and of comprehending humor, there are in fact differences between the two.

In general, it can be said that in order to recognize an incongruous situation, we must first be able to recognize a situation of congruity; that is, we must be acquainted with the reality in which stimuli are suited to past experiences and/or logical thought. A child who has never seen a dog will look at a five-legged dog without seeing it as something strange and unusual. For him, it is simply a new stimulus to be investigated and assimilated into the world of his environment. To a child who has seen dogs and knows how they should look, the appearance of a five-legged dog would be an incongruous stimulus. Every new, unknown stimulus creates curiosity in the child, who may react with laughter or with fear. Under what circumstances is either reaction caused?

In one of the classic experiments of psychology, Watson (1930) — the father of behaviorist theory — demonstrated how anxiety originates. Believing that most of our reactions are learned, and that learning is accomplished through a process of association, he conducted an experiment with the help of a little boy named Albert, who was 11 months old at the time. I conducted a similar experiment, which has probably been tried by many parents before me. This experiment was done with a child I call "Ari" after Aristotle, from whom I took the basic idea. Let us look briefly at these two experiments.

Watson decided to show how anxiety could be caused among children through the use of conditioning. He believed that only a certain number of stimuli naturally create fear in children, and that a sudden loud noise is one of these. He decided to pair with this unconditional (i.e., natural) stimulus a new, conditional one: Little Albert was presented with a white mouse. He touched it, petted it, and seemed quite happy playing with it. After a few such trials, Watson decided to activate the unconditional stimulus. One morning when the white mouse was brought to Albert, he touched it and a sudden loud noise (a hammer striking a piece of iron) was introduced. He was shocked by the noise and immediately left the mouse alone. When he calmed down, the mouse was again brought to him. Again, he tried to touch it; again, the frightening noise came; again, the child was scared and quickly pulled his hand away. After a number of repetitions of the conditioning process (the connection created between the noise and Albert's touching the mouse), the little boy's relation to the mouse changed drastically. Every time they showed it to him, he burst into tears and tried to get away from it. Furthermore, similar stimuli, such as a piece of white fur or a bit of cotton wool, aroused the same reaction.

So that the father of behaviorist theory should not be thought of as a sadist, it should be added that through the same method of conditioning Watson succeeded in curing Albert of his fear, and by the end of the experiment he was once again playing happily with the white mouse.

What about little Ari? Aristotle wrote about 2,500 years ago, "What causes laughter is something ugly but not painful or destructive. Take, for instance, the mask; it is ugly and distorted but does not cause pain." I used this principle for the experiment with Ari. I knew Ari, and the sight of me did not evoke any special response from him. One day I approached him with a smile on my face. Then I contorted my face as much as I could. Ari's glance showed suspicion — or was it curiosity? I quickly changed my facial expression to a broad smile. Ari's face changed too, and he began to smile. Thus a number of grotesque faces changed into smiles brought about smiles and then laughter in the child.

I asked some friends (male and female) to conduct this sort of experiment with their children, and they all reported identical results. You might try it, too; it's a good way of making a child smile. It's even better if you move your face from side to side while smiling, for movement greatly pleases babies.

Among older children, another child's making faces — a sort of "mask" — causes laughter and great enjoyment. They know that this "mask" is not dangerous. Children learn quickly that they can make others laugh in this way, too. The one who picks up the technique with particular speed and does it effectively becomes a clown.

A sense of fear was created in little Albert by the association of neutral stimulus (the white mouse) with a frightening stimulus (the noise). A response of enjoyment, expressed by laughter, was induced in little Ari through the association of a strange-looking stimulus (the grotesque face) and a clear signal that it was not dangerous (the smile). As the child develops, his world is broadened, and his intellectual capacity for perceiving the meaning of the stimuli he encounters is broadened as well. The fear of tangible objects and situations diminishes with increasing age, and the child's concurrent intellectual development brings him the ability to cope not only with the tangible, but also with the abstract. At approximately 2 years of age, he begins to relate not only to objects and persons in his surroundings, but also to things in his imagination. He creates an imaginary world. In his book *Play, Dreams and Imitation in Childhood* (1951), Piaget describes how the fantasy ability develops in children. He tells how, at the age of 1 ½ years, his daughter Jacqueline sat and pretended to eat. There was no food in front of her and no spoon in her hand, but she went through all of the motions of eating in a clear and complete fashion. At a similar age, his second daughter made the motions of brushing her teeth, using a finger as though it were a toothbrush. Piaget gives many such examples of pretending and notes that in most cases these activities are accompanied by a smile and laughter. By substituting movement and imaginary thought for real objects, the child creates a situation of incongruity; the incongruity and its resolution cause laughter.

This is actually the basis of children's play. As he develops, the child gains the ability to create an imaginary world, and his play is generally accompanied by enjoyment and laughter. His increasing mastery of the real world, like his mastery of the imaginary world, causes enjoyment accompanied by smiles and laughter.

In Chapter 1, I mention Hobbes's explanation of laughter as due to a sense of our superiority "by comparison with the infirmity of others, or with our own formerly." Children whose thinking ability is at one stage of development will laugh at other children who are at an earlier stage. A 5-year-old who can count from 1 to 10 in the correct order is transported with amusement when he hears another child, aged 3, count "1, 3, 7, 4." A 7-year-old bursts into wild laughter if an adult shows difficulty in solving a problem such as 2 + 2.

Similarly, a child's mastery of language rules leads to hilarity when another child uses words in an incorrect fashion. Simple word games, which greatly amuse children, reflect their sense of mastery of language rules. All of this explains why the reasons for children's laughter are completely different from those for adults; this is also probably why Freud thought that children do not have a sense of humor, and why we adults are amazed to see what things children find funny. Accordingly, it also explains why children do not understand what we adults find amusing.

The connection between the strangeness of a phenomenon and the response to it is found among adults as well. Like the reactions of children, our reactions to a phenomenon can range from apathy to anxiety and disquiet. Let's take an example: Someone demonstrates a card trick. If he is like most people (i.e., ordinarily clumsy), his trick will be very transparent and will evoke apathy on the part of an observer. Now suppose that another person, a little more talented, presents a different piece of conjuring. He cuts a deck of cards in front of the observer's eyes and shows him one uncovered card. He asks him what he sees. The observer answers, "The five of diamonds." The magician says, "The next card will be the eight of hearts." He hides the deck behind his back and cuts again. And what a wonder — the open card really *is* the eight of hearts. The magician announces that the next card will be the king of spades. And so it is. This trick causes curiosity: How does the magician do it? If the observer is smart enough he will discover the trick, which is actually very simple. Half of the deck is positioned facing the observer, and the other half faces the magician, who simply glances at the card facing him and cuts to bring it to the front of the deck, and so forth. The observer's discovery of this evokes laughter or a smile, because his success in solving the problem has proven that nothing strange or inexplicable is going on. The enjoyment stems from the solution of the incongruity that has aroused his curiosity.

Now let's suppose for a moment that the person doing the trick is none other than Uri Geller, the famous psychic. He presents a very complicated card trick that arouses the observer's curiosity, but with all his intellectual effort he simply cannot understand what Geller has done and how he has done it. When the observer turns to Geller and asks for an explanation, he swears that no trick is involved — simply a phenomenon connected with his supernatural abilities, which break the laws of reality as these are presently understood. Like other supernatural phenomena in the parapsychological field, Geller's achievements cause disquiet and even anxiety. This is because the incongruity between what the observer sees and the laws of nature as he knows them is inexplicable. The only way for the observer to keep from experiencing anxiety in this case is for him to presume that the laws of nature are still behaving as usual, and that he simply has not succeeded in unraveling the trick concerned.

The relationship between the strangeness of a stimulus and the reaction to it is shown graphically in Figure 5.1.

The coming into being of an incongruity represents a challenge whose solution highlights the intellectual function of humor. The enjoyment of understanding something is at the foundation of the humorous experience. But to this understanding another element may be added — that of release from regular thought and the bonds of logic. The humorous message raises a problem that we must solve, but the problem in humor is different from a problem in rational thinking, which is worked out logically and leads to a logical result. In humor this is not necessarily so. Humor has a logic all its own, which I have

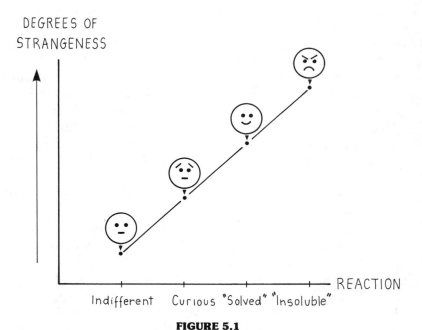

FIGURE 5.1

labeled *local logic* (on the analogy of *local patriotism*). I explain this concept in more detail in Chapter 6.

The incongruity of humor creates absurd situations, which of course lack logic. In order to enjoy it, one has to be ready to accept absurdity and to take momentary leave of Aristotelian logic. Consider this joke, for instance:

> *A passenger asks the bus driver, "What time is it?"*
>
> *"Thursday," says the driver.*
>
> *"Oh, I should have gotten off at the last stop."*

What actually amuses us here? Simply the trampling upon the laws of logic and the entry into another world, where logic does not control us as it does in all aspects of our everyday life. Humor is a signal that absurdity can be accepted and even enjoyed. If the joke with the passenger and the bus driver were to appear in a psychology textbook describing schizophrenic thought, it is doubtful whether we would laugh at it. Ionesco's plays, Lewis Carroll's stories, and Heller's *Catch-22* (1961) all make use of absurd humor.

Bergler (1956) contends that our intellectual enjoyment of absurd humor is an expression of revenge against our parents and teachers, who have prescribed for us how we should think and speak. Through our use of nonsense and investing of words with different meanings, we become omnipotent. As Lewis Carroll wrote in *Alice through the Looking Glass,* "When I use a word, its meaning is what I choose, no more and no less."

In addition to the release from reason that humor provides, it has a further intellectual function — that described by Koestler (1964) in his explanation of the creative process as a process of bisociation. *Bisociation* is the formation of an original link between different elements of two situations — the establishment of a new meaning. Koestler contends that humor as well as creativity is based on bisociation. Connecting two frames of references in an unusual way can create a new theory in science or a humorous situation. In humor, a situation in which each of two people follows his own frame of reference can create something that is "funny" in both senses of the word: "bizarre" or "amusing." A nice example of such a situation is illustrated in Figure 5.2.

Bisociative humor, as opposed to absurd humor, gives new meaning to a situation that at first does not appear to be very meaningful:

FIGURE 5.2

St. Peter, the gatekeeper of heaven, asks someone to take his place for a few minutes. Jesus himself takes up guard, and suddenly someone knocks at the gate. It is an elderly, decrepit man, who turns to him and says, "I'm an old carpenter. I once had a son whom I loved very much, but he disappeared. I've been all over the world, and I've asked people if they've seen my son, and they all said they'd heard of him and know about him, but have never met him. Maybe he's here?"

With tears of excitement welling from his eyes, Jesus opens his arms and exclaims, "Father!"

"Pinocchio!" cries the old man and embraces him.

And another example of bisociation appears in Figure 5.3.

In summary, the intellectual function of humor enables us to enjoy the workings of our intellectual capabilities. Intellectual humor reflects our broadening understanding as it increases with maturity. It enables us to create as well as to solve problems in an enjoyable fashion, since we know that these are not problems that demand an "effective" solution. The intellectual aspect of humor grants us temporary freedom from the bonds of rational thought, an escape to the absurd, and a return to childhood games in which fantasy occupies a more honored position than logic. And finally, it is a creative process in which we put together problems that demand solution by means of different frames of reference. Understanding this sort of humor requires that we take into account different aspects of a situation that are not necessarily connected with one another at first glance.

All these aspects of the intellectual function of humor are what cause us enjoyment. When we offer a humorous message in which the intellectual elements discussed are clearly present, we amuse our listeners. Their enjoyment stems from the activation of their intellectual processes and the insight that they achieve. And one of the main motives for communicating a humorous message is probably to enjoy the enjoyment of others.

In summarizing the object of the *functions* of humor, it is important to emphasize that my definition of five functions is artificial and arbitrary. Of course, there are "pure" forms of humor that fulfill a single function of humor in an unambiguous way. In each chapter of Part

FIGURE 5.3

I, I have given instances of jokes that exemplify the function under discussion. But there *are* jokes that fulfill more than one function, and there are some that fulfill most of them. The best way of ending this chapter and this section is to give an example of this last type of joke:

> *After 5 years of analysis, the psychiatrist informs his client that he is healthy and can get married. He does so, and he and his bride go to spend their wedding night in a hotel. Upon their arrival, the groom goes into the bathroom. The bride waits and waits. After an hour, she puts her ear to the door and hears him murmuring, "I have to remember: This is not my mother — not my mother — not my mother."*

The sexual function is probably the most obvious aspect of this joke, it also contains elements of aggression toward a person in a role of authority (the psychiatrist), defense against anxiety, and intellectual arousal through the lack of congruity at the end of the story.

Now that I have clarified the main functions of humor, I move on to Part II, which deals with the techniques, content, and situations of humor.

II

TECHNIQUES, CONTENT, AND SITUATIONS OF HUMOR

How is humor produced? Are there specific techniques? Can one create humor by using them? For some people, humor is indeed no more than the application of a few techniques that provoke laughter. One of these is the use of incongruity. Philosophers of the standing of Kant and Schopenhauer have explained laughter as resulting exclusively from incongruity. In a frequently quoted little phrase that I come back to later, Kant wrote that the source of laughter is "the sudden transformation of a strained expectation into nothing." In other words, when one expects something and gets nothing, one will laugh. This should be explained to all gamblers in Las Vegas and elsewhere, whose strained expectations very frequently turn into nothing. Perhaps, instead of becoming frustrated, they might feel like laughing?

There is no doubt that incongruity is a necessary but not a sufficient cause of laughter. So many elements in fact coexist in humor that one has to take account of different techniques in order to understand some of its complexities. As the discussion of humor's intellectual functions in Chapter 5 indicates, a sense of incongruity provides the motivation for "solving" a joke. But to resolve incongruities, one can either use logic or employ a different mode of thinking. The particular way of approaching incongruity in humor is what I call *local logic,* and it is in my view the key to understanding and enjoying humor.

I use the joke as a model for understanding what goes on in our heads as we listen to a piece of humor. Comprehending our mental processes may help us to see why we laugh and enjoy a joke. A theoretical model is proposed here in the clear knowledge that, like most models related to any aspect of human behavior, it is not all-inclusive and certainly not perfect. Even if it were, it would still not help much in the creation of jokes. A model is in some ways similar to a cookbook. A person may have all the ingredients and follow the instructions faithfully, but more than ingredients and instructions are needed to make a good cook. Culinary talent cannot be learned from a book; neither can a sense of humor. But a cookbook can help a bit — and I think that a joke model can add to our understanding of humor.

There are of course many forms of humor besides jokes, and different techniques are used to create them. Some of these — certainly not all of them — are presented here in brief. I try to show that they all involve some common elements that appear in the model.

After the discussion of the techniques of humor (the *how* one creates it), the next question covered — in the shortest chapter of the book — will be *what* one uses. What are the topics of jokes, comedies, satires, and other forms of humor? Are there specific kinds of subject matter (or content) that are considered fit for jokes, while others are taboo? For some people, religion, homeland, or motherhood — to give just a few examples — are no laughing matters. My own views on the possible topics of humor are also made clear.

Finally, I consider the question of *where* humor is produced. Are there specific situations where humor blossoms freely? As becomes apparent in Chapter 8, it may appear in many unexpected places, but there are definitely some situations where it is unwelcome. Certain group structures and the climate in them can encourage or discourage uses of humor. Sad situations, as well as special moods induced by life events or by drugs or alcohol, also influence the appearance or nonappearance of humor.

I turn now to these three aspects of humor: techniques, content, and situations.

6

The Techniques of Humor

The question of how humor is made takes us to the work of the humorist. Those who create humor (and most of us do, now and then) use certain techniques; this is true for those who create spontaneously, as well as for the professionals. The techniques of humor are varied: Some are rather simple, while others are fairly complex. The person who consistently creates humor is a rather special one, and later chapters of this book are devoted to his personality. For the time being, let us try to understand the techniques used in humor creation.

INVOLUNTARY AND VOLUNTARY HUMOR

First, let us differentiate between *involuntary* and *voluntary* creations of humor. Involuntary humor is created when the person responsible for other people's laughter has no intention of making them laugh. Such involuntary humor can be either visual or verbal. In the visual variety, someone who slips on a banana peel, or who fails to realize that his fly is open while he is making a serious proposal about the necessity of doing something about people's low morality, makes us laugh. These people certainly do not want to do what they do. Uncoordinated physical movements, such as sitting down not on a chair but beside it, also have a funny effect. Obvious incongruities of physique, as in a couple where the man is small and skinny with a thin voice and the woman is huge and baritone-voiced, likewise produce involuntary humor. Of course, one can voluntarily imitate such forms of involuntary humor, and many actors do it rather successfully.

Involuntary humor can also be verbal. Sometimes slips of the tongue can be funny. So are the naive remarks of children, who do not mean to be humorous.

> *A little girl asks her mother where babies come from. As a progressive parent, her mother describes the whole process, from intercourse to the development of the fetus for 9 months and the enlarged abdomen that results, and finally birth itself. Shortly after, her plump, elderly spinster aunt calls, and the child says, "You've got a swollen tummy, and I know why!"*

Involuntary naiveté displayed by adults is amusing too, of course, and it may also be put on deliberately to raise a laugh.

I do not deal further in this chapter with involuntary humor; it only amuses accidental bystanders. Of primary interest here is the creation of humor arising from the conscious effort directed toward making the "audience" laugh. I mention involuntary humor only because it gives rise to one technique for creating humor: The voluntary imitation of involuntary humor can be used to create situations that make people laugh.

FORMAL AND INFORMAL HUMOR

There are two types of voluntary humor: *formal* and *informal*. *Informal* humor means the kind of remarks made spontaneously in a given situation that make other people laugh. This is the most common form of humor, occurring under natural conditions and furnishing our main daily supply of laughter. Throwing off a funny remark that puts a familiar state of affairs into a new light indicates a fair degree of competence in humorous creation. To this category belong teachers who can infuse wit into their explanations, politicians whose speeches are relieved by humor, and people who in ordinary conversation can seize upon and present new perceptions in a funny way.

Formal voluntary humor is generally the property of professional humorists. It is the result of serious and deliberate work and is intended for presentation. People who make up jokes, or those who write comic plays, sketches, or films, are creators in a very real sense; few engage in such creation without conscious effort. Joke *tellers* do not actually display creative ability, though some creativity may in fact be necessary to be able to produce the right joke at the right moment. Moreover, the talent for acting that may contribute to success in telling jokes does not necessarily indicate *humorous* creativity, as the same talent can assist a tragic actor or the defense counsel for a murderer.

The kind of voluntary humor that displays creative ability can take many forms. Like any other message, the humorous message can be expressed in different ways and can be taken in by different senses. In psychology, the senses are generally divided into *primary* and *secondary* senses. Sight and hearing belong to the first category, while taste, smell, touch, and so on belong to the second; most humor is directed toward the primary senses. The techniques for conveying a humorous message vary with the senses to which the techniques appeal. Visual types of humor include physical, nonverbal, and verbal humor. Physical humor is based on bodily movement that arouses laughter, as in pantomime. Nonverbal humor appears mainly in graphic form and includes cartoons. Visual verbal humor means humor in written form — joke collections, funny articles, and the like. Verbal humor can also have an aural aspect, as when comic actors and entertainers follow a written script. Finally, there is an aural mode of humor that is less widely recognized but is just as enjoyable: musical humor. Mixed media, such as television and the movies, can of course use all these forms in combination.

TECHNIQUES FOR CREATING HUMOR

Let us now discuss briefly the techniques for conveying humorous messages in different media, restricting the discussion to formal humor. (Formal humor can be analyzed; informal humor has to be enjoyed in its context.) I use cartoons here as an example of visual humor, and jokes as an example of verbal humor. Analyzing the joke form permits the construction of a model for the basic elements that appear in most forms of humor.

Techniques in Cartoons

First, however, a few words on cartoons are in order. A cartoon works through symbols — simple notations that represent complex ideas. Its basic principle is to present its message pictorially and as economically as possible. It exaggerates certain features and sets up a lack of congruity, either internally (in the cartoon itself) or between the picture and its caption. Symbols like Uncle Sam for the United States or a bear for the USSR allow the caricaturist to minimize his dependence on words and explanations. The stereotyped Jew of the Nazi caricaturists (black hair, humped back, big nose) was used to suggest the hateful and destructive role of the Jews in world politics.

When a well-known person is caricatured by the exaggeration of one of his features, he begins to seem ridiculous. This is how a cartoonist expresses aggression toward him. Grotjahn (1966) feels that a cartoonist resembles a witch doctor in a way. He writes:

> In addition to using overemphasis of detail to degrade, [the cartoonist] also seeks to gain power over the victim of his aggression by old, abandoned, infantile methods. As [in] primitive societies, where the witch creates a doll and uses it, by magic, to gain power over the person the doll represents, so the caricaturist hopes unconsciously to regain this magical power in his cartoon and to destroy his enemy with it. (p. 152)

Not every cartoon is aggressive, of course, for all the other functions of humor described in Part I can also find pictorial expression. Figure 6.1, for example, shows how a cartoon can act as a defense mechanism against anxiety.

Another technique used by cartoonists is the creation of incongruity among a picture's components. Such cartoons exemplify in a way peculiar to themselves the intellectual function of humor; their conflicting elements set us a problem that amuses us if we can solve it, and leaves us at a loss if we cannot. Figure 6.2 demonstrates the creation of incongruity within the elements of a cartoon. Incongruity may also be set up between a picture and its caption. In a cartoon by the English caricaturist Victor Breeze, for example, we see the following:

> *A company director is leaning back in a large chair behind an enormous desk. An old man in work clothes is coming into the room, holding a mop in one hand and a pail in the other. The company director turns toward him and says, "Don't listen to all that talk about getting jobs through relatives, Daddy."*

FIGURE 6.1

Here it is relevant to ask what the special quality of a cartoon is. If a funny situation can be described in a few words, the addition of a graphic element is not always worthwhile; a picture should not be a *substitute* for language. Some cartoonists, indeed, confine themselves to pictorial images. When we read in the papers about the problems of the economy, for example, a cartoonist might sketch the government official in charge of finance as a hospital patient whose temperature is surging upward on a chart. Though this would be a rather abstract treatment, it does not display much creativity or graphic invention. The best cartoon is one that in a single picture shows a situation that would require many words to describe, and even then might not seem funny. Figure 6.3 is an example of such a cartoon. Try to describe this cartoon verbally and see how long it takes, and whether listeners find it as funny as those who just look at the picture do.

Special talent is required for the creation of cartoons. Everyone

FIGURE 6.2

enjoys cartoons, and everyone is capable of enjoying and can sometimes create verbal humor; however, very few can express humor by
means of a cartoon, which calls for good drawing ability as well as
the gift of compression.

Techniques in Jokes

I now move on to verbal humor, whose most common form is the joke.
In jokes, the main elements of humor appear in a concentrated manner.

> *A young man looking for a wife went to a computerized marriage
> agency. Filling out the form, he wrote, "I'd like someone who likes lots
> of company, water sports, and formal dress, and is preferably rather
> short." The agency sent him a penguin.*

This story contains the basic constituent of all humor, one that is necessary although not sufficent: surprise. There is no laughter without surprise. As noted in the introduction to Part II, Immanuel Kant wrote more than two centuries ago that "laughter is an affection arising from the sudden transformation of a strained expectation into nothing." I would like to call this the theory of "frustrated expectation." In every form of humor, the audience is led in a certain direction and encouraged to form certain expectations, and these are then turned upside down. In this sense, the humorist leads people astray, and if they want

FIGURE 6.3

to enjoy themselves they must let it happen. This calls for a particular state of mind, a playful readiness not to take things too seriously and to accept impossibilities as possible. A person who is always serious will not only not enjoy humor, but will probably be angry at having been tricked into wasting time on pointless rubbish that has nothing to do with "real life." Playful readiness in addition to surprise is another necessary (but still insufficient) condition of humor.

Not every surprise, of course, leads to laughter. Frustrated expectation may arouse indifference, anger, or fear. We all know that there are plenty of unpleasant surprises in life, and that they are not funny. My daughter Michelle made this clear to me when she was 13. We were discussing humor, and I asked her what makes people laugh. She said, "The unexpected — but not any unexpected thing. If, for instance, we are sitting here and we hear from the next room a lion roaring and we look and see that it's only a mouse, we will laugh. But if we hear a mouse squeaking and we look and see a huge lion, that won't be funny, that will be scary!"

The surprise in humor, as my daughter well understood, should not be threatening. (As I note in Chapter 5, Aristotle proposed this idea many years ago.) Not only should the surprise not be threatening, it should be in some way bound up with the context of the joke, even if the connection is not very logical; the joke about the marriage agency and the penguin is a fairly good example. However, there is some kind of logic involved here — something I call *local logic*.

Like local patriotism, local logic is appropriate only in certain places. In humor, local logic is appropriate in a way, because it brings some kind of explanation to the incongruity. We wait for one thing, and we get another thing that is quite different but that nevertheless has a certain suitability. If, for example, the marriage bureau were to have sent the young man a horse, that would be extremely surprising, but not funny. Sending a penguin, on the other hand, *does* seem funny; although it is not at all what he is expecting, it in fact fits all his requirements — all but one, which he does not write down, and which is perfectly evident to us as well. The local logic is very amusing if we are willing to play along, but not if we say crossly that marriage bureaus do not send penguins to their clients.

This story illustrates another necessary factor in humor — the short time span. Every joke must have a punch line, a point of climax that is quickly over. Shakespeare knew it; he wrote in *Hamlet* that "brevity is the soul of wit." The length of the joke itself does not matter, but the actual funny part must be short. One does not laugh all the way through a comedy, but only now and then at brief climactic moments. In his book on the art of the cinema, Jerry Lewis noted that laughter must have its proper "dosage": "You have to let people rest after a good laugh, give them time to calm down and prepare for the next laugh" (1962, p. 142).

There are many techniques for creating humor, but all involve surprise, incongruity, and a short time span. Theoreticians of humor all mention particular techniques, especially, of course, those most relevant to their theories. Bergson (1899/1975), for instance, gives many examples of the techniques of imitation — certainly a most efficacious technique, and one much used by entertainers looking for "safe" effects. An Eskimo speaking with a German accent, or a Black person with a Hungarian accent, seems funny to the audience. Many entertainers have built dazzling careers on their imitations of political figures. What is so funny about such imitation? First, it produces surprise, and, second, it displays incongruity.

Bergson also stresses the use of mechanical behavior, such as the constant repetition of a phrase, which turns it into a catch phrase. "Can I do you now, sir?", endlessly repeated on the radio program *Itma*, swept hilarity throughout Britain in the 1940s.

Freud has given special weight to techniques of wordplay — an emphasis arising from his interest in slips of the tongue, which play an important part in his theory, and in words that express symbols. Among the many forms of wordplay is the use of slight word changes, as in Tom Lehrer's "She makes coffee that tastes like cham . . . poo" ("shampoo" instead of the expected "champagne"). The use of words with double meaning, as in this joke, is another form:

> *A doctor visits a sick woman and says quietly to her husband, "She doesn't look good to me."*
>
> *"You're telling me!" says the husband: "She hasn't looked good to me for 20 years."*

Freud (1905) illustrates not less than 20 different humorous techniques, most of them based upon wordplay.

Another well-known and useful technique is switching from one level to another. Words that generally have an abstract sense, for example, seem funny when given concrete realization. Imagine this cartoon:

> *Two politicians are in conversation, and one says, "One just can't talk*
> *to Smith these days — he sees Communists under the bed everywhere."*
> *In fact, two colonels who are obviously from a Communist country are*
> *lying flat on the carpet under the desk.*

Here the surprise resulting from incongruity stands out clearly, as it
does in the technique of divergence from the context. This joke is an
example of such divergence:

> *A husband comes home and finds his wife in another man's arms.*
> *"Now I know everything!" he cries.*
>
> *"Oh yes?" says his wife. "So who was the 13th President?"*

Another example of switching levels is the technique of role change,
as when a patient cures the doctor or a student gives his teacher an
examination; yet another is the technique of internal contradiction,
as when someone says of himself, "I am intelligent, handsome, witty, tolerant, and, above all, modest."

The technique of the absurd is illustrated in Chapter 5 and satire
is discussed in Chapter 1, which also deals with the strategies of humor and with the difference between primitive and sophisticated humor. These, together with what is discussed here, are some of the principal techniques of creating humor. Of course there are others, but
all share the factors of surprise, incongruity, and brevity.

The model about to be introduced illustrates the intellectual and
emotional processes that explain our enjoyment of humor. Like every
psychological model, it is incomplete, and any inventive reader will
find modes of humor that it cannot explicate adequately. Future research will almost certainly enrich and improve it, but even in its present state it will help us in the understanding of some main points in
the process of humor enjoyment.

A COGNITIVE-EMOTIONAL MODEL
FOR THE COMPREHENSION
AND ENJOYMENT OF HUMOR

This model is primarily intended to explain our enjoyment of jokes,
but its central elements can also explain our enjoyment of cartoons
and humorous remarks. The joke has been chosen because it is a for-

mal and well-known mode of humor. The model comprises six main stages: preparation, the joke's content, tension and violation of balance, the cognitive process, cognitive enjoyment, and functional enjoyment.

Preparation

Frequently, but not always, a person telling a joke or saying something funny indicates that what he is about to say is not to be taken seriously. This makes it easier for the listener, who knows that he must switch to a "playful" frame of mind — that is, that the message is not "for real," and that he should be ready for something that will not necessarily develop in a logical way and that will make him laugh. Thus preparation helps to create the right atmosphere. Among its recognized forms are the following:

1. *The social situation.* This has a considerable influence. When someone gets up at a party where jokes have been told for the last half hour, the readiness to laugh is such that almost anything he says will seem funny.

2. *The humorous image of the speaker.* This means our evaluation of the speaker as a humorist on the basis of past experience. The mere appearance on the stage of a famous comic arouses laughter, and in any group of friends there will be some who are known as "jokers."

3. *Comic appearance.* External appearances indicate the nature of a thing. When we see a circus clown with his huge red nose and chalky face, we look forward to laughter. Even if he says nothing, his very shape and baggy clothes prepare us for amusement. The look and walk of Groucho Marx or Jerry Lewis emphasize the comic effect before they open their mouths.

4. *Facial expression.* Smiles, laughs, or facial contortions also prepare the listener for a humorous message in what he is about to hear.

5. *Verbal declaration.* Expressions such as "I've got a great joke to tell you," or "Did you hear the one about . . . ?" or "In Woody Allen's last movie . . . " all give promise of something funny to follow.

Each of these different forms of communication signals to the listener that a funny message is coming, and calls on him to "change gear" from seriousness to playfulness. The more signals, the greater the expectation. If there are more than three such hints, people may collapse with laughter before the joke has even begun, and hints have a cumulative effect of their own, creating a climate (social situation) in which there is laughter almost without the pretext of jokes.

Such hints can be viewed in a hierarchy from the most simple to those over which the joke teller has really no control: (1) verbal declaration; (2) facial expression; (3) humorous image; (4) comic appearance; (5) social situation. The stage of preparation benefits the joke teller because it creates a suitable atmosphere, but there are also dangers in it. The expectation aroused may be so high that a joke that would otherwise have amused people merely disappoints them.

Spontaneous funny remarks generally have no preparation. Some comedians deliberately keep a straight face and give no hints, and this actually increases our pleasure when we discover the humor for ourselves, with surprise thrown in.

The Content of the Joke

Most jokes have three stages: the establishment of the background, a story that leads the listener in a certain direction, and the punch line. The last is the most important, giving rise to surprise and frustration of the expectations formed in the two preceding stages. The absence of congruity creates surprise, which signals the beginning of the third stage in the model.

Tension and Violation of Balance

People feel discomfort and tension when they encounter an incongruity; for example, the inability to solve a puzzle creates tension. If you want to establish this for yourself, take some paper and try to solve this problem. Three houses stand in a row, and there are three utility lines (gas, electricity, and water) to be laid down for each. The lines may be laid down in any way, but they must not cross. Copy the sketch shown in Figure 6.4 and use it for the problem. When you have tried and failed, copy it out again and keep trying. For those who wish to feel to the full the tension arising from the inability to solve an apparently simple problem, I suggest 15 minutes' work on it; after this, turn to p. 98. The stubborn (or persistent) among you can go on as long as they like. If you go to sleep after working a certain time on the problem and failing to find the solution, elements of it will probably appear in your dreams. (I should be very grateful to any reader who would care to write me about such dreams.)

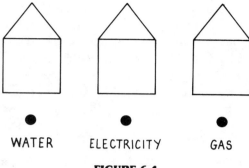

FIGURE 6.4

Intellectual tension is created not merely when one tries to solve a problem, but when there is a lack of balance among the elements of a situation that is the result of an illogical or unexpected connection among them. Here is a situation with three elements:

1. John loves Mary.
2. Mary loves flowers.
3. John sends flowers to Mary.

There is a logical connection among these three elements; they are in a "balanced" relationship, without any conflict, and the situation is clear and rational. The third sentence is explained by the first two.

Let us imagine a different situation with the following elements:

1. John hates Mary.
2. Mary loves flowers.
3. John sends flowers to Mary.

Here a lack of balance is created. The third sentence is not only not explained by the first two, but it sets up a question: Why should anyone send flowers to someone he hates? Since we cannot see clearly what is happening, we are spurred on to think of some explanation. If we add a fourth sentence —

4. Mary is allergic to flowers.

— the situation becomes "balanced" and comprehensible. That extra sentence is the outcome of the tension always felt when a system is not in equilibrium — a condition that Festinger (1957) calls "cognitive dissonance." Cognitive dissonance is characterized by the attempt to reorder a system so that its balance returns. Thus the surprise aroused by a humorous message creates a lack of equilibrium and intellectual tension, and these lead to the model's next stage, that of comprehension and enjoyment.

The Cognitive Process

The cognitive process aims at understanding and "solving" an incongruity, thus restoring balance. The idea that listening to a joke involves thinking may seem strange, for a punch line seems to arouse immediate laughter without any time for reflection. But this is not so. Each word we hear goes through a conceptual process in the mind, the result of which is to give it meaning. This is done so rapidly that it doesn't seem to take place at all, but it does. What happens in our minds when we hear the punch line of a joke?

First of all, we feel that "there's something wrong here." We have expected one thing and have found another. We are accustomed to logical thinking, and all of a sudden it does not work. Failing to solve a joke's incongruity by logic, we try the thought mode of local logic. If at first (the stage of preparation) we have had a hint that a joke is coming, we shall probably try at once to operate in the field of local logic. Anyone who stays with ordinary logic will not understand or be amused by the joke, but will arrive at another "balance" — that is, "This is illogical, and there's no point in trying to make sense of it." Someone who is not so consistently rational, but who can move from seriousness to playfulness and can adjust his mode of thinking to match, will find a solution and so will reach the fifth stage of the model.

Cognitive Enjoyment

Cognitive enjoyment is the feeling of satisfaction that comes from resolving a joke's incongruity. Basically, it is a release from tension, and it finds physiological expression in laughter.

Functional Enjoyment

Functional enjoyment derives from the pleasure that a joke gives by fulfilling a specific function for the listener. People may enjoy a joke about sex, for example, because it enables them to touch on sex with-

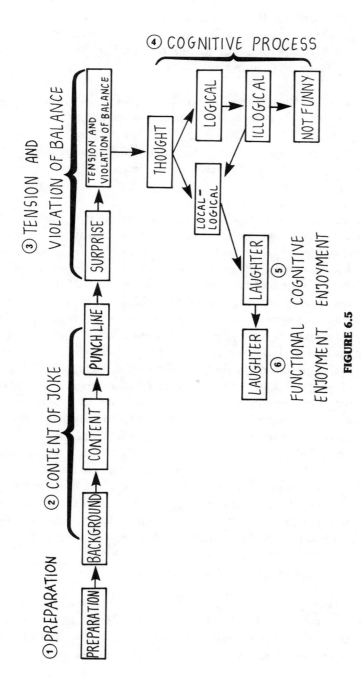

① PREPARATION

② CONTENT OF JOKE

③ TENSION AND VIOLATION OF BALANCE

④ COGNITIVE PROCESS

PREPARATION → BACKGROUND → CONTENT → PUNCH LINE → SURPRISE → TENSION AND VIOLATION OF BALANCE → THOUGHT

THOUGHT → LOGICAL → ILLOGICAL → NOT FUNNY

THOUGHT → LOCAL-LOGICAL

LOCAL-LOGICAL → LAUGHTER ⑤ → LAUGHTER ⑥

FUNCTIONAL ENJOYMENT   COGNITIVE ENJOYMENT

FIGURE 6.5

97

out incurring social disapproval; aggressive jokes are amusing in the circumstances described in Chapter 1; and so on. In most forms of humor, our laughter has a double source, arising both from cognitive and from functional enjoyment.

Figure 6.5 shows the whole model graphically. In order to understand the model better, analyze the following joke:

I had a terrible dream last night. I dreamed that scientists had finally found a way to exploit the sun's energy completely — and then the Arabs bought the sun.

It can be seen that there is a central place in this model for what I have called *local logic,* which occupies a middle position between logical and pathological thinking. In the former, the rules of logic are in continuous control; the problems dealt with and the solutions found are all on a realistic plane; and there is no room for fantasy or comprehension of the absurd. Pathological thinking, on the other hand, is characterized by a separation from reality, and its conceptual processes take no account of the rules of logic. Fantasy and the absurd are in control and are perceived as reality.

Local-logical thinking uses and enjoys both logic and fantasy without confusing them, and offers solutions that involve one or the other as required by the context. An inclination towards humor calls for paralogical thinking of this sort, if one is to comprehend and enjoy both the world of reality and the world of imagination.

In concluding this chapter, I should like to make a wish: that its readers should not allow to happen to themselves what has happened to me. From my researches into humor and analysis of its techniques, I sometimes find that instead of enjoying new jokes I take them apart to see whether they fit my model. Laughing less at jokes is a heavy price to pay for scientific knowledge. But there is one compensation: Serious matters now make me laugh more.

[**AUTHOR'S NOTE:** The solution to the problem on page 94 is that there is no solution. This problem is impossible to solve. I do hope, dear reader, that you are not frustrated, but that you did feel the tension I have described while trying to find the solution.]

7

The Content of Humor

This is the shortest chapter of the book, since in fact any topic can be subject matter for humor. The simplest way of giving a full list of the possible subjects of humor would be to print the *Encyclopaedia Britannica* as an appendix.

It is important to distinguish between the *content* and the *function* of humor. In discussing humor's functions, I have noted that a joke whose content is sexual may actually fulfill aggressive, social, or defensive functions. The same is true of political or religious jokes. This chapter, then, deals only with content and not with function.

I have said that any and every subject can serve for humor, and this is what life itself seems to show us. There is a kind of unwritten law guaranteeing freedom of humor. Most Western countries give legal protection to freedom of speech, but nothing can ensure it beyond the shadow of a doubt. And just as there are those who try to destroy it, so too, unhappily, there are those who are against freedom of humor, who hold that there are some subjects too serious or sublime for laughter. These subjects, even for some humorists, are taboo: Religion is considered off limits in some cases, the state in others, and so on.

Where do specific taboos come from? One source is certainly a person's world view. A religious person who never mentions God's name lightly will be shocked if it is laughed at, and will think that jokes about religion are not funny but blasphemous. This does not, of course, prevent other people from making such jokes. For example, in the academic world, a cartoon that functions as a defense against the fear of examinations depicts God as an examination candidate:

In the picture, the earth is hanging in space; there are two tiny figures on it — Adam and Eve — with a tree between them. A little above the earth is an old man with a long beard and halo, pointing down proudly. Above him is an older man with a longer beard and a larger halo, who is saying, "And for work like that you should get a doctorate?"

If religious people had enough power, "religious" humor might be banned. At the time of the Inquisition, a joke like the one given above could have led one to the stake, and I very much doubt whether anyone risks jokes about Islam in the Iran of Khomeini. In Eastern Bloc countries, similarly, where Communism is a kind of state treasure, mockery of the party ideology is sternly forbidden (and, as noted earlier, "underground" humor with an important social function arises in consequence). But there may be surprising individual exceptions to this rule. In his book on humor and politics, Albert Sauvy (1979) describes a reception at one of the embassies in Moscow at which the following joke was told by Khrushchev himself:

> *A man stands in the middle of Red Square and shouts out, "Khrushchev is crazy! Khrushchev is crazy!" Within seconds the secret police arrive and he is arrested. At his trial, he gets 3 months for disrespect toward the party leader, and 10 years for revealing a state secret.*

Some people feel that it is wrong to laugh at the state or motherhood or any other "sacred" subject, and anyone whose world view gives a central place to such a subject will regard it as taboo for humor. Personal identification with a particular group or area of life can have the same effect. People who endured the horrors of the Holocaust are shocked by jokes about it. Jews detest anti-Semitic jokes (when told by an anti-Semite). And traumatic experience can set up at least a temporary taboo. A person who normally enjoys black humor but who has just lost a friend will probably recoil from jokes about death.

The prohibitions on certain subjects, even if understandable in the light of people's beliefs or feelings, constitute a limitation on our freedom to grapple with our problems. If those who believe in sacred cows could bind others to respect them, we would be in a bad way. Imagine the huge posters that would appear in lecture halls: Laughing At Religion Is Prohibited! Laughing At Capitalism Is Prohibited! Laughing At Sex Is Prohibited! Laughing At Irishmen Is Prohibited! Laughing At Death Is Prohibited! . . . or perhaps just Laughing Is Prohibited! Happily, people do feel free to laugh, and if one group rejects a given topic another will find it funny. *Chacun à son goût* (each to his own taste) is the rule in cooking: No one thinks of forbidding a particular taste, whether it is sweetness or saltiness or acidity. So too, in humor, one cannot really argue about what is funny, and any subject is legitimate if it does in fact make people laugh.

It should be said that some subjects seem to be preferred by different age groups. Small children are highly amused by references to elimination and the sexual parts, the very mention of which will make them howl with laughter. When they go to school, the content of their jokes becomes richer and more varied, and technique rather than subject matter becomes prominent (McGhee & Chapman, 1980). They laugh mainly at wordplay and riddles. In adolescence, the content is still more varied, and humor may be detected in almost any subject. For adults, as Chapter 2 indicates, sex constitutes the most common topic. But in general, the subjects for humor are coextensive with the subjects for human thought.

8

The Situations of Humor

In this chapter, I discuss the influence of situation—the "where" and "when"—upon the creation and enjoyment of humor. Environment is of decisive importance for arousing or dampening expressions of humor. Places that have a dampening effect are those with tragic associations for an individual or group: cemeteries, terminal wards, Christian churches on Good Friday, and so forth. Attendance at a funeral and contact with the bereaved family take away any urge to be funny, for they make us face not only the death of a specific person but the idea of our own death. As Chapter 4 indicates, death can serve as a topic for black humor—but not when we are freshly and personally confronted with it.

Judaism (and, in other ways, other religions as well) tries to ease the transition from the depression following bereavement back to normal functioning. For a week after a funeral, the family members remain at home and are visited by their friends and relations, and this gives them an opportunity to emerge gradually from their preoccupation with the death and to begin to take an interest in other subjects. It may happen that over the 7 days the topics of conversation lighten somewhat, and that by the end there are even some sparks of humor. Persuading a mourner to smile may help him considerably in coping with the death. Humor can also appear in hospitals and, as we have seen, can help patients to face acute illness, though the more serious their condition is, the less humor can do. It does most for patients who think positively about recovery and the return to a normal life. For them, it is generally self-disparaging humor that helps them cope best.

Visitors in a hospital ward are often afraid to use humor, not knowing how the patient will react. But if the patient himself makes a funny remark or responds with a smile to one of theirs, he is signaling his readiness to listen to humor, and in such cases it may be a real help. Humor from the doctors is an even greater psychological aid. Moody (1978) has devoted an entire book to the healing power of humor, showing with numerous examples how it contributes to the process of recovery. Sometimes a sick person in a hospital may use humor to dispel the anxiety of a visitor. At the same time he encourages himself by making the hospital a transitory place for everybody. As a sick friend told me once when I visited him, "Who comes and visits? Potential patients. It's good you come — it gives you a bit of practice for the time you'll be a patient here." This remark possibly cheered him up, but it didn't help me much. In fact, visits usually enliven the patient and depress the visitor, and some patients try to inspirit their visitors with humor whose basic message is "It isn't so bad."

A synagogue on Yom Kippur, or a church on Good Friday, constitutes an environment that extinguishes humor. Happily, there are festive days as well.

As against these depressing circumstances, there are both formal and informal environments that encourage humor. "Formal" ones include places of comic entertainment — comedy theaters, night clubs, and so on — where humor planned in advance is presented for payment. The people who go to such a place know what to expect, and this expectation plays a part in the show's success.

Social meetings of different sorts constitute "informal" environments for humor, where not the setting but the social situation is the important factor. Humor in a social situation is created within the interpersonal system that develops or has developed among the people present. In groups with a common way of life, humor forms part of that life — a phenomenon discussed at length in Chapter 3. I can now discuss another aspect of this phenomenon: the frequency of humor in relation to the sexual composition of a group. Sherman (1975) carried out systematic observations of children in kindergarten, and found that heterogeneous groups (boys and girls together) laughed more than homogeneous (single-sex) groups. He explained this finding in terms of the richer stimulation that is characteristic of interaction between the sexes; he also asserted that in a heterogeneous group there is greater sexual alertness and that this alertness encourages laughter.

Among adults, it is the subject matter of humor that is principally influenced by a group's sexual composition. In an all-male group, sexual humor takes pride of place, whether it is sophisticated or vulgar. If a woman appears, the sexual content becomes more refined. In all-female groups, the content is different and the humor is less aggressive or sexual, though the feminist movement is changing all that.

Women feel less obliged to be "ladies," and they talk more freely about sex; these changes probably also influence the kind of humor they enjoy. Chapman and Gadfield (1967) found that activist women are more amused by jokes in which a man is depicted at a disadvantage than nonfeminist women are.

But, in any case, humor flourishes more in mixed groups, owing to a fact that is discussed in detail later on — namely, that men are better at creating humor and women at enjoying it. The women's laughter stimulates the men to be more amusing; furthermore, Sherman's remarks on the greater sexual alertness in heterogeneous groups of children apply to adults as well. The atmosphere of a group also influences its humor. Humor abounds more where the atmosphere is democratic (i.e., where people see one another as equals) than where it is authoritarian. Coser (1960) showed that in a hierarchical structure humor is the privilege of those higher up on the ladder, and in the classic study of Levin, Lippit, and White (1958), it was found that children under authoritarian supervision play less and express less humor than children under a "democratic" regime.

Membership in social groups characterizes our lives. Each one of us belongs to many such groups, whether by choice or compulsion. (Friends, for example, constitute an optional group, and the army constitutes a compulsory one.) As shown in Figure 8.1, social groups can be placed along two axes: formal-informal and compulsory-optional. The extent to which a group encourages humor can largely be determined by its position in relation to the two axes. In general, the freer the atmosphere is of compulsion or of formality, the more humor will manifest itself. As formality increases, the group requires that relationships be conducted in accordance with a hierarchical structure, and this limits free expression of humor and thus humor itself. As the degree of compulsion increases, furthermore, a person's relationships with the other members of the group become more constrained; he cannot leave even if he dislikes them personally. It might be expected, therefore, that richer self-expression is to be found among the members of a group on the left-hand side of the continuum. Actually it is not so simple, for groups influence not only the *quantity* of humor, but also (and primarily) the functions it fulfills, its content, and even its techniques. I illustrate this here with reference to one such group, the army.

An army is a model instance of a social group with a formal structure. Its relationships are characteristically hierarchical and unyield-

FORMAL

COMPULSORY

OPTIONAL

INFORMAL

FIGURE 8.1

105

ing; every soldier knows who can give him orders and who must take his. In such conditions, at least three situations that encourage humor are created. First, there is the kind of humor that tends to strengthen the hierarchy — jokes created or told by the highly placed about or to their subordinates, who feel that it is their duty to laugh. There is also the humor that arises among equals, such as is found in all groups. Finally, there is the "underground" humor that attacks the high ranks and cannot be uttered in public. Privates imitate and ridicule their officers behind their backs. The functions of humor are also influenced by the different situations. Underground humor can serve both aggressive and defensive functions, while humor among equals has mostly social functions.

Membership in a group naturally influences the subject matter of humor as well: "Army" jokes develop in the army, drawing both on its life and on its particular slang. Techniques, too, are influenced. The "concrete" humorous techniques characteristic of children reappear in the army, for soldiers, like children, are in a situation of almost total dependence upon authority. The infantilism sometimes found in soldiers comes to expression in their humor.

This brief discussion of army humor should make it easier to understand the particular humor of other groups located at different points in relation to the two axes.

Besides our participation in social groups, we also belong throughout our lives to age groups, from kindergarten to retirement homes. In every such age group, humor arises from the circumstances specific to it. High-school humor is different from maternity-ward humor, and both differ from the humor in an old-age home, to give a few of the many examples. Another type of group, one in which there is not necessarily any direct interaction, is the professional group. Doctors, lawyers, taxi drivers, and laundry workers all find themselves in situations that are specific to their work and out of which humor develops — humor that is meaningful only to those in the know. "Professional" humor's subject matter is rooted in the form of work in question, and it can fulfill any of the standard functions of humor. Doctors and psychiatrists can serve as an example. Members of this professional group constantly interact with those who are sick in mind or body; their contact with human tragedy arouses in them tension and, frequently, anxiety. Doctors in surgical wards tell black jokes to one another (though not to the patients or visitors) because such jokes offer release from tension and are a defense against the anxieties induced by the work. The same process operates among psychiatrists. One of the most popular jokes among psychiatrists is as follows:

> *After 2 years of intensive treatment, a psychologist says to his patient, "Now I can tell you for certain that you don't have an inferiority complex. You are just inferior."*

For the psychiatrists who tell this story to one another, it is a joke against themselves that serves as a defense. Told by someone else in a different situation, it would be an act of aggression.

In Chapter 6, I discuss the importance of mood in grasping and enjoying a humorous message. In most people, moods vary according to circumstances, and it is easy to tell when someone is feeling good. In this state, he is more receptive to messages that can enhance it; his mood is a magnet for stimuli that will strengthen it, humor among them. His readiness both to create and to accept humor also lowers his critical threshold, so that a mediocre joke amuses him more than it does when he is in a bad temper. A critical threshold is a kind of strainer whose meshes widen as a state of mind improves. At his happiest, a person finds almost any kind of humor acceptable; even if he generally likes only sophisticated wit, custard-pie slapstick may then find favor. In a really bad mood, by contrast, he may refuse to find anything funny at all.

It is different when the *creation* of humor is in question. Bad mood in a creator of humor may give rise to genuine humor of a specific type, usually aggressive or cynical. One of Israel's best-known satirists told me in an interview that his main satiric motive was his gloom at Israel's situation. One of the characteristics of a good mood, furthermore, is its missionary aspect, the desire to share one's enjoyment with others — and here the social function of humor comes into prominence.

While mood is admittedly influenced by circumstances, it may also be influenced by artificial means, of which alcohol is the most striking example. Laughter comes more frequently and strongly from persons with a few glasses of liquor inside them. In addition to improving mood, alcohol reduces the alertness of the central nervous system, especially of the cortex. Since the cortex is responsible for rational thinking, its temporary weakening allows for an increase in irrational and pararational thinking; I note in Chapter 6 that pararational thinking (local logic) is essential to the comprehension and enjoyment of humor. As someone once said, "The superego is the part of the personality that is soluble in alcohol."

I learned in a striking manner of alcohol's beneficial effect upon humor when I gave a seminar to top-level executives in Paris; as an exercise, I asked the participants to relate amusing incidents at work. Until lunch, the exercise went on ponderously and with minimal laughter. During lunch, which of course was accompanied by good wine, people continued to tell stories; the more they drank, the more everyone joined in, and the louder and more continuous became the laughter.

Everyone knows from experience or hearsay that alcohol improves the mood. We often say to a friend who is looking gloomy, "Come on, let's have a drink." This knowledge is not merely individual but cultural or national, for on public holidays like the Scottish Hogmanay (New Year) or the Jewish Purim, everyone is encouraged to drink to create a festive atmosphere.

How about drugs? Schachter and Wheeler (1962) carried out a laboratory experiment of the effect of drugs upon mood and enjoyment of humor. Three groups of students were injected with two kinds of drugs. One group received epinephrine, a stimulant; the second chlorpromazine, a tranquilizer; and the third slightly salted water, which has no effect. The students did not know what they were getting. An excerpt from a comedy film was then screened. Those who had been given a stimulant laughed more and reported the film more often as amusing than did members of the control group (the third one), who in turn laughed more and were more amused than members of the tranquilized group.

In sum, then, a person's mood, no matter how created, influences the degree of pleasure he obtains from humor.

A few words should be added on special situations. States of crisis or emergency, such as war, elections, and natural or economic disasters, give rise to humor that uses them as its subject matter and tries to grapple with the tension they generate. Such humor is primarily aggressive, but may also function as a promoter of social cohesiveness or as a defense mechanism against anxiety. A line popular in Israel at a time of heavy emigration typifies the cohesive/defensive function: "Last one to leave, turn the light off."

So much for the connection between situation and humor. Part III deals with personality characteristics and their relation to the enjoyment and creation of humor.

III

HUMOR
AND PERSONALITY

Having discussed the "why" (functions), the "how" (techniques), the "what" (content), and the "where" (situations) of humor, I now turn to the question "who." In other words, I seek to clarify the relationship between humor and personality. And in order to clarify this relationship, I begin in Chapter 9 by looking into the two main dimensions of humor: its creation and its appreciation. In addition, a theory of personality is described and then used to examine the relationships between humor and personality.

Those who enjoy humor—namely, most of us—have certain preferences. While some enjoy aggressive or sexual humor, others prefer intellectual humor. For some, black humor is highly enjoyable; for others, it is distressing, and certainly the topics of black humor are not obviously laughing matters. In Chapter 10, I attempt to define personality differences among people who enjoy different functions of humor. My contention is that people enjoy different forms of humor because their needs differ, and that people's needs stem from their personalities. Another aspect related to humor appreciation and personality concerns the quantitative aspects of laughing at humor. There are those who search for humor and express their appreciation by laughing. Others do not enjoy humor and very rarely laugh. These forms of behavior are also related to personality, as I indicate in Chapter 10.

Who are those who have the gift to make us laugh? Do their personalities differ, from those of people not blessed with this talent, and, if so, in what ways? We all know and admire professional humorists. Those who write books, humorous articles, and comic screenplays create humorous situations that make millions laugh. So do gifted cartoonists. Comedians and stand-up comics are even more popular; they attract huge audiences to theaters, movies, and shows. Doubtless they have a very special talent: They know how to make us laugh. These are the professional humorists, and they can be divided into creators of humor and performers of it. But we all know that they are not the only ones who have the gift of making us laugh. There are other people with such gifts, who are not professionals and for whom humor creation is something to be used in social interactions. I call them "amateur" humorists. These people are generally well liked by their peers, because they can give pleasure by making them laugh. But they may also be feared, for humor, as we have seen, can be a dangerous weapon.

Professional humorists are well known, being in the limelight of publications and performances. But what about the amateurs? They are generally known only among their friends and/or coworkers. How can we discover them for research purposes? A special methodology can be devised to identify them. After "discovering" them, one can compare them with their nonhumorist peers. Are their personalities different from those of their nonhumorist peers? In what ways are professional humorists similar to amateurs, and in what ways do they differ? Are there particular family backgrounds typical of humorists? What are their views on humor? These are some of the questions I clarify in Chapters 11 and 12.

9

Dimensions of Humor and Personality

Some people enjoy humor more than others. Some, in fact, are able to make others laugh frequently. These are not just "joke tellers"; they are individuals who can perceive and enjoy situations in a special way and can communicate their perceptions in ways that make others enjoy them as well. Their enjoyment is expressed by smiling or laughter. Some of us are mostly appreciators and enjoyers of humor, while others are more gifted in creating it. Let us look at these two ways of relating to humor.

THE TWO DIMENSIONS OF HUMOR

In the introduction to this book, I offer a brief definition of the main dimensions of humor: *humor creativity* and *humor appreciation*. I can now go into more detail concerning these dimensions. *Humor creativity* has been defined as the ability to perceive relationships between people, objects, or ideas in an incongruous way, as well as the ability to communicate this perception to others. This communication can be verbal and elicits in others smiling or laughter. We know now that the incongruity in humor follows its own type of logic, local logic, as explained in Chapter 6.

Humor appreciation has been defined as the ability to understand and enjoy messages containing humor creativity, as well as situations that are incongruous but not menacing. To this, I can now add that humor appreciation is a function of the ability to adopt local-logical thinking, and that humor enjoyment can be cognitive and emotional.

These two dimensions of humor can be thought of as being situated on two orthogonal axes. The horizontal axis represents the appreciation of humor; the vertical axis, its creation. Everyone can be placed in a particular position in relation to the two. The left-hand end of the horizontal axis represents the person who never laughs (this, in fact, is hardly possible for a normal human being). As we move to the right, we encounter people who laugh increasingly often — people who find more and more things funny. We need not concern ourselves with the extreme right-hand end of this axis, for apart from some very rare pathological cases, there is no one who laughs all of the time.

The vertical axis, as noted, indicates the capacity to create humor. At the bottom of this axis comes the person who hardly knows how to do this. He may be able to repeat a joke, but cannot invent one; people who ruin punch lines belong here. We ascend through greater degrees of creative competence to the unusually gifted near the top of the axis; this level includes professional humorists such as Woody Allen or Art Buchwald.

How can we situate people in relation to these two dimensions? First, let us explain that humor appreciation, as well as humor creativity, can be measured. I have myself constructed a humor questionnaire, which is described in detail elsewhere (Ziv, 1979b, 1981). On this questionnaire, the degree of agreement with statements like the following makes up the score of humor appreciation:

When others laugh, I generally join the general laughter.

I find many situations funny.

Comparing myself with my friends, I enjoy more the jokes I hear.

The degree of agreement with statements like the following makes up the score of humor creativity:

My friends expect me to make them laugh.

When I want to stress a point, I frequently use humor.

Of course, other measuring instruments have been devised to quantify people's degree of humor appreciation and creativity. Some of them are briefly described in the discussion of humor creativity in Chapter 11.

In order to clarify how persons can be situated in relation to the two dimensions of humor, let us look at some examples (see Figure 9.1). X is a person who loves to laugh and laughs frequently. He loves

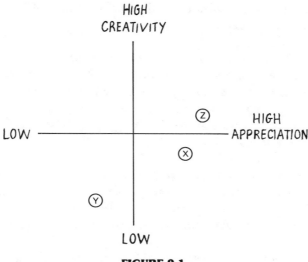

FIGURE 9.1

comedies and is considered a merry person by his friends. Now and then he creates humor: He makes others laugh by showing the funny side of some situation. Y is a serious person; he laughs very seldom and considers life too serious to waste his time on "nonsense" things. He is rather critical toward those who laugh and joke, and he never indulges in making humorous remarks. Z is an agreeable person who loves laughing and looks for occasions to do so. He also loves to make witty remarks and frequently tells jokes appropriate to the situation.

Each person can be situated at a particular point in relation to the two dimensions, as shown in Figure 9.1. Research shows that most of us are situated in the lower right-hand quadrant: We enjoy laughing, but we do not create much humor.

Let us now turn to personality.

WHAT IS PERSONALITY?

The definitions of personality are as numerous as the theories about it. Psychoanalytic theory gives rise to definitions that are totally different from those based on learning theory. While every theory takes a different approach, most would probably concur with the classic definition of Allport (1956) because of its sheer comprehensiveness: "[P]ersonality is the dynamic organization within the individual of those psycho-physical systems that determine his unique adjustment to his environment" (p. 47).

The real problems in the investigation of personality begin when we try to pin down the separate components by which it may be described and measured. A glance at all the attempts that have been made to do this can make us despair of ever comprehending personality. The efforts of those who have tried to investigate personality can teach us the following:

1. One needs tremendous patience and almost superhuman persistence in searching for the elements composing personality.

2. Extremely sophisticated and complex statistical techniques seem only to establish facts that have been intuitively known for over 2,000 years.

3. The more one investigates the central elements of personality, the closer one comes to the semantic origins of humor.

Let us take a brief look at the researchers' efforts to find the main components of personality.

In 1936, scientists extracted from the largest unabridged dictionary of the English language all terms used to describe personality. No fewer than 18,000 were found. Of these, they selected the ones describing relatively permanent character traits and modes of behavior; this selection narrowed the field to about 4,500 terms (Odbert & Allport, 1936). Cattell (1957), an expert in the statistical method of factor analysis, grouped these terms into 171 categories, which on further analysis yielded 41 pairs of characteristics that were thought essential to the description of personality. More statistical work and consultation with judges (experts on personality) reduced the list to 24 — that is, 12 pairs of contrasting terms, such as "talkative-quiet" (Cattell, 1957).

Another researcher started from the same list of 4,500 qualities and arrived at five factors (Norman, 1963). In the wake of dozens of studies using complex statistical procedures, Eysenck and Eysenck (1969) have concluded that personality should be considered in relation to four central factors constituting the end points of two axes. In describing their four basic personality types, the Eysencks have noted that they correspond to the types delineated by Hippocrates (the founder of medicine in ancient Greece, who lived about 2,200 years ago).

The Hippocratic types were based on the theory that a person's health and character were a function of the combination of the "humors" or fluids in his body. (This is the origin of the word *humor*.) An excess in anyone of the four humors (blood, black bile, yellow bile, and phlegm) was thought to give rise to a specific kind of temperament: blood to a "sanguine" temperament, characterized by self-confidence, cheerfulness, and sociability; black bile to a "melancholy" one, tending toward depression and pessimism; yellow bile to a "choleric" one, irritable and aggressive; and phlegm to a "phlegmatic" one, passive and apathetic.

European medicine depended on the theory of humors until the end of the Middle Ages, and traces of it still exist in language — for example, in the French *bonne humeur* and the English "good humor." *Humor* acquired its modern sense only in the 17th century. To conclude this minireview of personality research, we can say that "humor" was already considered the core of human personality in ancient Greece.

In trying to reach a better understanding of the relationship between personality and the enjoyment of humor — that is, what sorts of people enjoy which sorts of humor — we must not think about isolated characteristics of personality, but about general theories. I have chosen the Eysencks' from the many existing theories, for two reasons. First, this is a modern theory, economical and elegant in its terms. It has been empirically investigated by psychological as well as physiological research. In addition, it is not tangled in a multiplicity of nebulous terms. Second, it highlights the ancient but ever new connection between humor and personality.

It is evident to me, as it is to the Eysencks and as it should be to all theoreticians in the field, that there is no question of a perfect model that can explain everything and every personality. However, the Eysencks' theory does provide a clear economical framework that allows for good research approaches. I briefly outline the theory here and then add to it an important element.

Most personality variables can be described and related to one another through the use of two axes, as noted. One of these is the *social axis* — the continuum for a person's relations to others. The Eysencks use the terms *extroversion* and *introversion* for the end points of this continuum. Extroverts seek relationships with others, while introverts avoid them. Most people, of course, are located somewhere in the middle of this axis, with one tendency more or less dominant, as might be expected from a normal distribution.

What are the personality traits of those on the "extroversion" end of the continuum? The typical extrovert is very sociable, with many friends and a need for social interaction. He likes parties and noise, is eager for stimulation, takes chances, and acts impulsively. He generally feels good; he is optimistic, quick to react, and fond of change; he is active and inclined to be aggressive. The typical introvert is usually quiet and rather closed in himself, preferring books to people and shying away from social contact other than with close friends. He is inclined to be introspective, makes long-term plans, and does not react impulsively. He likes an orderly life and does not readily express emotion or lose his composure. He is rather pessimistic and avoids large, noisy social occasions.

Let me again stress that "pure" extroverts and introverts are rare. The former may sometimes like to be alone, just as the latter sometimes need company. An introverted person who normally never joins in the conversation may suddenly be aroused to passionate speech when Nicaraguan stamps (or whatever else he is interested in) are the topic of the moment — that is, he may behave like an extrovert.

The Eysencks' second continuum concerns man's emotionality. At one end of the scale is the extremely emotional person; at the other is the very stable one. The highly emotional pole has been labled *neuroticism* by the Eysencks — an unfortunate choice because of its pathological connotation. I prefer to call the two extremities of the emotional axis *stability* and *emotionality*.

As with extroversion and introversion, most people are distributed around the midpoint of this axis. The emotional type expresses his feelings openly, crying and laughing as appropriate. His moods change quickly; he is easily hurt and prone to anxiety. Small things arouse him, such as a sentimental movie or a wild flower. The stable type is the opposite. He is of a cold temperament; he does not show when he is hurt; he remains calm even in situations of stress; and his feelings, whether of love or hate, are not easily read.

Important and characteristic personality traits can be placed in relation to the Eysencks' two continua by the Cartesian method, as I have done for the two axes of the appreciation and creation of humor (see Figure 9.1). Is this system sufficient for describing personality? On the whole, yes, since significant traits can be related to the two axes and also to one another. The closer together two traits are, the higher the correlation between them is, while an angle of 180° indicates a negative correlation. Figure 9.2 shows the Eysencks' axes, together with examples of traits. (One can also see from the figure how surprisingly the Hippocratic character types merge into a modern theory.)

To the two essential dimensions of personality defined by the Eysencks — the social dimension of introversion-extroversion and the emotional dimension of stability-emotionality — a third should be added: the cognitive dimension. Unfortunately, for historical reasons, there is a clear dichotomy between psychologists doing research in personality and those interested in the intellectual aspect of the individual. Research in intelligence started systematically with Binet's creation of his famous objective measuring instrument. The IQ concept became central in psychology, and literally thousands of research projects were conducted, using more and more sophisticated intelligence tests. In spite of many criticisms directed at the tests, they are certainly the best instruments devised by psychologists. Their predictive

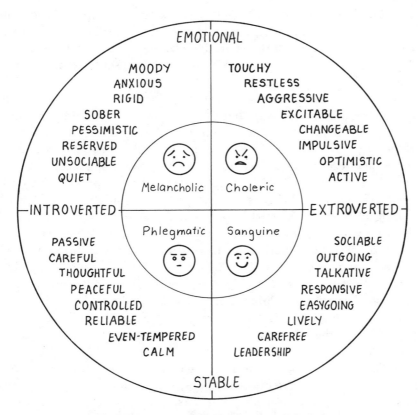

FIGURE 9.2 (ADAPTED FROM EYSENCK)

value for educational achievement and problem-solving abilities has no match in the psychological armamentarium. However, psychologists interested in the intellectual functioning of individuals have ignored personality differences in most cases. This is true of those doing research in the measurement of intelligence, as well as of those studying the development of thinking. Piaget's contribution to understanding children's thinking is doubtless tremendous. However, he studied his subjects as problem-solving beings, ignoring personality differences among them. On the other hand, psychologists studying personality have developed countless theories, concepts, and measuring instruments, but for the most part have ignored intellectual differences among individuals. When one thinks of such giants in psychology as Freud and Piaget, one wonders how each ignored the other's field of interest. It seems as if Freud developed a psychology without intelligence and Piaget one without a soul.

There is no doubt that intelligence is an important component of personality, and to ignore it is to miss something essential. Let us see how the addition of the cognitive elements (i.e., intelligence) to the two personality dimensions defined by the Eysencks enriches our understanding.

Two highly extroverted persons with different levels of intelligence will express their extrovert characteristics in a very dissimilar manner. I have mentioned that one main characteristic of extroverts is their sociability. One can sagely assume that a highly intelligent extrovert can easily become a leader; with a low level of intelligence, chances are that an extrovert will be a follower. They both express their social needs, but do so in different behaviors. A highly intelligent introvert will probably be interested in books and may even write some. An introvert with a low level of intelligence will probably just keep to himself and try to find interest in simpler things. Similar differences in behavior should be obvious even when we combine both of the Eysencks' dimensions with intelligence. Therefore I should like to suggest a model with three dimensions — social, emotional, and cognitive. Each dimension represents a continuum of behavior, and each is independent of the others; in other words, these are three orthogonal continua.

To make the model clear, let us take the introversion-extroversion axis first. As I have mentioned, there is a "normal" distribution on this continuum, which means that most people have both extrovert and introvert tendencies. Tests can determine the degree to which they are found in any given person. Example 9.1 gives examples of the questions used in such tests.

There are similar questionnaires measuring the emotional dimension of personality. As for the cognitive one, the well-known intelligence tests may be used. For all three dimensions, we find the general population distributed according to the laws of the normal curve. Statistical procedures elicit the percentage of the population to be found

---

EXAMPLE 9.1
Introversion-Extroversion

Hundreds of questionnaires have been devised to measure the social dimension of personality. The following questions reflect introversion-extroversion:

Do you like to spend a lot of time with others?	Yes/No
Do you generally prefer reading to meeting people?	Yes/No
Do you generally need friends to improve your mood?	Yes/No
Do you feel uncomfortable with people who like practical jokes?	Yes/No
When you are with other people, do you tend to talk a lot?	Yes/No
Do you like to be by yourself for long periods?	Yes/No
Do you form friendships easily?	Yes/No
Do you feel uncomfortable on entering a room full of strangers?	Yes/No
Is it important to you that many people should like you?	Yes/No
Do you avoid large groups of excited people?	Yes/No

If you answered "Yes" to the odd numbers and "No" to the even numbers, you have a score of 10, which means that you have strong extrovert tendencies. If you answered "No" to the odd numbers and "Yes" to the even ones, you have a score of 0, which means that you have strong introvert tendencies. Scores therefore vary between 0 and 10, so that a low score indicates a greater or lesser degree of introversion, and a high score indicates a greater or lesser degree of extroversion. In this way, a single number can describe one's position on the social continuum.

However, do not attempt to diagnose yourself on the basis of these 10 questions. They are only intended to give an idea of the sorts of behavior typical of introverted and extroverted people.

in each section of that distribution. The stanine method divides the normal distribution into nine parts, as shown in Figure 9.3.

As explained in Example 9.1, low scores in the social dimension indicate introvert tendencies, while high scores indicate extrovert tendencies. Thus a score of 2 here denotes an introverted person, and a score of 9 denotes an extremely extroverted one. On the emotional dimension, low scores indicate a stable person, while high scores indicate an emotional one. Finally, on the cognitive dimension, low scores denote low intelligence (1 = mental deficiency), while high scores denote high intelligence.

The three-dimensional model that I propose can be depicted by means of three axes, each of which starts with 0 and is divided into nine sections. A person's position on each one can be determined by social, emotional, and intelligence tests. Let us imagine four different persons, whose scores on three dimensions of personality are as follows:

	Personality Dimensions		
Person	*Social*	*Emotional*	*Cognitive*
A	9	4	6
B	2	8	8
C	3	3	4
D	3	3	9

A is extremely extroverted, fairly stable as to his emotions, and a little above average in intelligence; B is quite introverted, extremely emotional, and very intelligent. You can fairly well describe C and

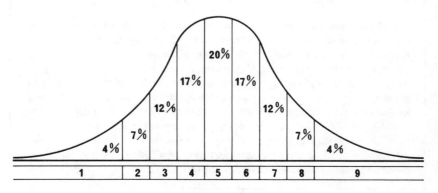

FIGURE 9.3

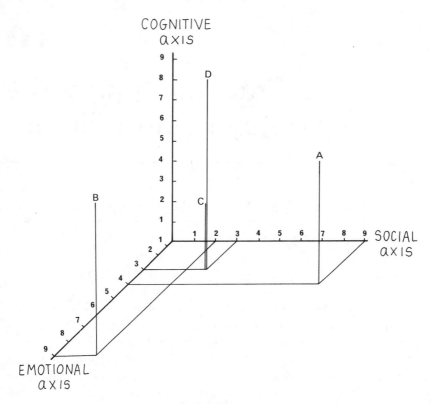

FIGURE 9.4

D, who are similar on the social and emotional dimensions, but different on intelligence. Certainly their behavior will be rather dissimilar, due to the differences in their intellectual level. Please pay attention to the fact that even if we confine ourselves to only three dimensions of personality, we can describe no fewer than 723 personality types with the use of stanines!

The three-dimensional model of personality can be represented by a cube, with each person situated at some point in the interior space of the cube. This model can be two-dimensionally represented as shown in Figure 9.4.

Now that we have a theoretical framework for personality as well as for the two dimensions of humor, the relationship between humor and personality can be clarified. First, I discuss personality and humor appreciation.

10

Personality and the Enjoyment of Humor

"Right! I've had enough! Tomorrow I'm just not going to school any more, and I'll give you two good reasons: The kids hit me back, and all the teachers are nasty to me."

"I'm sorry, but tomorrow you will go to school, and I'll give you two good reasons: You're 48 years old, and you're the principal."

If you are laughing at this joke, you belong to a certain group. If you are not laughing, don't be concerned: You belong to another group, and undoubtedly laugh at jokes of another sort. Like any other joke, this one gives rise to different reactions: "That's great," "It's infantile," "What's funny about it?", and, as Queen Victoria said, "We are not amused." But remarks of this sort are less important than behavior — the response of laughter. The best way to judge the degree of a person's enjoyment is to examine his laughter. Some people laugh frequently and others very rarely, and it is reasonable to assume that the former enjoy humor more.

One reservation on the issue of "quantity" of laughter should be noted: In all areas of human behavior pathological conditions exist, and some cases of hebephrenia are characterized by almost continuous laughter that does not arise from any humorous stimulus. The same is sometimes true of severe mental deficiency, while in acute depression the patient may not laugh at all. But, setting these extremes aside, we can say that the frequency of laughter is a measure of the degree of enjoyment derived from humor.

In this chapter, I attempt to clarify the relationship between personality and humor appreciation by looking first at quantitative and then at qualitative aspects of laughter.

WHO LAUGHS AND HOW MUCH?

The quantitative question can be answered quite easily. People located nearer the "extroversion" end of the social continuum derive more pleasure from social interaction, and since spontaneous humor flourishes mainly in social groups, it is reasonable to conclude that extroverts enjoy humor more than introverts. In Chapter 3, I have noted that humor strengthens group cohesiveness. The need of extroverts for social reinforcement finds satisfaction in the shared enjoyment of humor. I have also noted in Chapter 3 that someone who laughs at a group's jokes is more readily accepted by it — something that matters to the extrovert. Pleasure in the humor supplied by others increases the motivation to seek their company. Thus, for the extrovert, humor is an important means of satisfying his social needs.

What is the relationship between the social axis and the emotional axis in regard to this question? Extroverted and stable personalities enjoy humor more, so that *emotional* extroverts will have less pleasure, because their emotionalism may set up barriers to humorous messages whose subject matter might provoke anxiety. Hence the combination of high extroversion with low emotionalism gives the greatest enjoyment.

How about those who enjoy humor less? In general, they are to be found nearer the "introversion" end of the social axis. Since introverts recoil from social involvement and prefer their own company, they have few opportunities for the spontaneous humor that arises within social interaction. Their efforts to protect their privacy and to avoid sharing their thoughts or experiences with others find behavioral expression in a tendency to take life's events with great gravity, and this tendency forestalls the playful mood that is one of the conditions for enjoying humor. Emotional introverts are the people who derive the least pleasure from humor — the melancholics, in the Hippocratic formulation.

What is the influence of the cognitive dimension? Setting the other two dimensions aside for the moment, we can say that people of high intelligence enjoy humor more, simply because they can grasp a greater number and variety of more humorous messages. Thus a stable and highly intelligent extrovert is in a better position to enjoy humor than a similar personality with low intelligence. Things are not so straightforward, however, since in a group where the humor is of the practical-joke variety (which gives no intellectual satisfaction), the stable extrovert of low intelligence will enjoy himself more than the one of high intelligence. Here I touch on the qualitative aspect of laughter: Who enjoys what sort of humor? But first let me again stress that the description given here, like all scientific descriptions, concerns probabilities and not individuals (i.e., it is a generalization). Of course there are introverts who have great enjoyment from humor and extroverts who have none; however, the distinctions I have drawn allow for a general understanding of the connection between personality and the quantitative enjoyment of humor. The results of my research support those theoretical views.

Before concluding this review of the quantitative aspects of humor enjoyment, I should mention two other findings. One is related to age; the second to sex differences. From my research (Ziv, 1979a) with adults and adolescents, I have found that there is a peak age for humor enjoyment: middle adolescence. The ages of 15–16 are very much "laughter-prone." Girls are then at the "giggling age," and boys are avid readers of such publications as *Mad*.

As for sex differences, women in general laugh more than men; they have higher humor appreciation scores than males. However, men make more jokes than women and are thus higher in humor creativity. These sex differences are explained in the discussion of humor creativity in Chapters 11 and 12.

The alert reader may notice that I have not ascribed the same importance to the three dimensions of personality in regard to the enjoyment of humor. There is, in fact, a hierarchy: The social dimension is the most decisive factor, followed by the emotional and (a long way behind) the intellectual. In the *creation* of humor, the elements of this hierarchy appear in a different order.

WHO LAUGHS AT WHAT?

The question of qualitative enjoyment of humor involves the different kinds of humor (i.e., different as to function, technique, subject matter, or situation) and the different kinds of personality formed by combinations of the three dimensions. In each dimension there are high and low levels, as shown schematically in Figure 10.1, which also

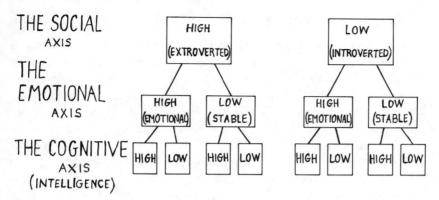

THE SOCIAL AXIS

THE EMOTIONAL AXIS

THE COGNITIVE AXIS (INTELLIGENCE)

FIGURE 10.1

observes the hierarchy of dimensions noted above. To simplify the discussion, I ignore the cognitive axis for the time being and concentrate on the two higher ones, which in combination yield four types — the emotional extrovert, the stable extrovert, the emotional introvert, and the stable introvert. At the risk of nagging (see also Figure 10.2), I must again repeat that this is a typology — that I am not talking about given individuals, but about what is broadly true of different personality types.

FIGURE 10.2

The Emotional Extrovert

Who is the emotional extrovert? I have already described extroverts as opposed to introverts, and emotional people as opposed to stable ones. What are the characteristics of the person who combines extroversion with emotionality? The picture emerging from the dozens of studies in this area (see Eysenck & Eysenck, 1969) is of a restless, changing, easily hurt person who is also aggressive, impulsive, optimistic, and active.

Humor satisfies two main needs in this person — to express his aggression in an acceptable way, and to be accepted by a group. Thus his favorite humor functions in aggressive and social ways, and he enjoys "ethnic" jokes because they involve aggression against an external group and strengthen his sense of belonging to his own. The intellectual function of humor matters less to him, and he will generally dislike humor that acts as a defense mechanism. Black humor does not give him pleasure, as its subject matter is likely to be pessimistic and to arouse anxiety. Only rarely does he turn humor against himself, and he does not understand how others can do so. In sum, he finds Charlie Chaplin much more amusing than Woody Allen.

As to technique, he prefers short jokes and spontaneous funny remarks, since these are generally aggressive or sexual. He will greatly enjoy practical jokes (unless he is their victim). Humor in written or cartoon form means little to him, while skits and comedy entertainment mean a great deal; and the laughter of the rest of the audience increases the pleasure he takes in comic performances. Most humorous topics and situations will strike him as amusing, and his impulsiveness enables him to laugh even in circumstances that are far from funny in themselves.

The Stable Extrovert

The stable extrovert is characteristically sociable, talkative, full of life, ready to initiate and respond to conversation, free of worry, and inclined to take things easily. Usually he is content with himself, confident in his powers, independent, and possessed of leadership tendencies.

Clearly, for such a personality, the social function of humor is central. He enjoys comedies greatly, because their rosy depiction of the world corresponds with his own views; he tends to regard satire's negations as unconstructive. Aggression (in a refined form) is important to his enjoyment of humor — the kind of critical but funny remark that oils the wheels of group interaction. He likes practical jokes even when he is their victim, and he is particularly fond of telling jokes himself, because they add to the social atmosphere and strengthen his image as a leader. He does not care for black humor with its grim world view; his self-confidence means that he can laugh at himself and can approve of others who do the same; and intellectual humor lets him express the playfulness of mood that fits his philosophy of life.

Like the emotional extrovert, he prefers verbal and presented humor, but his greater stability gives him the patience to enjoy longer humorous messages, and he is likely to enjoy cartoons as well. As to humorous situations and subject matter, he is more fastidious than the emotional extrovert: His awareness of social rules and capacity for self-control prevent him from laughing in inappropriate circumstances, and his sensitivity to others' feelings prevent him from laughing at ethnic jokes (for example) if someone present might be hurt.

The Emotional Introvert

The emotional introvert is given to changes of mood and a pessimistic view of life. He is anxious, rigid, unsociable, quiet, and closed, in general, he is not at all a cheerful person. As I have already noted, he derives less enjoyment from humor than any other personality type. If something does amuse him, it probably has an aggressive function; because of his gloomy view of the world, he approves of attacks on it. He also enjoys social humor, especially in the form of satire, for its social criticism. He may like black humor because it reduces his anxieties by making them seem funny; thus, *the lion shall lie down with the lamb . . . but the lamb won't sleep very well.* However, he probably rejects topics that cause him great anxiety as subject matter for humor. Since he is uncomfortable with social interaction, he prefers cartoons and written humor to its spoken or acted forms. For the same reason, there are relatively few situations in which he can enjoy humor, and his laughter will never be uproarious.

The Stable Introvert

The stable introvert is a calm type who very rarely loses his self-control. He is cautious and passive, planning everything beforehand and avoiding impulsive action. He likes humor best in its intellectual function: Absurd and incongruous situations amuse him immensely, and the problem-solving process involved appeals to him, principally because it provides renewed proof of his ability to arrive at a correct solution without the aid of others. He enjoys aggressive or sexual humor only if it is camouflaged and sophisticated, and he likes black humor because it is a distorted and absurd presentation of subjects normally taken seriously. In view of his capacity for presenting himself negatively (a very rare quality), he also enjoys humor against himself.

He tends to dislike the most common humorous topics, sex and aggression, just because they are common. As to technique, he prefers written forms, though acted humor also speaks to him. He is fairly fastidious with regard to situation, for he holds that the world is organized and rational and therefore that laughter is inappropriate in some situations.

The four personality types and their humor preferences are summarized in Table 10.1. These types, as noted earlier, are combinations

Table 10.1
Personality and Humor Preferences

Humor Category	Personality Type			
	Emotional Extrovert	Stable Extrovert	Emotional Introvert	Stable Introvert
Functions				
Aggressive	xx	x	x	
Sexual	x	x		
Social (general)		x	x	x
Social (interpersonal)	x	xx		
Defense against anxiety			x	x
Self-disparaging		x		x
Intellectual		x	x	xx
Techniques				
Written/cartoons				xx
Narrated or acted	x	xx		
Situations				
Numerous	xx	x		

Note. x indicates preference; xx indicates strong preference.

of the social and the emotional dimensions. How does the cognitive dimension affect the enjoyment of humor? Its principal effect is on technique, for intellectual level determines the degree of sophistication that one can enjoy. People of average or low intelligence tend to like jokes that require a minimum of effort to understand. They will (on the whole) enjoy practical jokes and custard-pie slapstick, which are (on the whole) not very popular to people of high intelligence. More intelligent people may appreciate simple-minded humor when in a playful mood, but their main pleasure comes from the problems set by sophisticated humor. Since all functions of humor can be mediated in a sophisticated or in a simple way, the extent of a person's enjoyment of humor that fulfills a given function for him is affected by his own and the humor's intellectual level.

To summarize: In this chapter, I have presented a two-dimensional theory of personality that is based upon the ancient humors as well as modern research; I have added to it a third dimension, that of intelligence. I have also made some theoretical suggestions as to the quantitative and qualitative pleasure in humor experienced by different personality types. I now approach the other dimension of humor: its creation.

11

Personality and the Creation of Humor

In the preceding chapter, I have discussed the people who enjoy humor, and have tried to illuminate the connection between personality and the enjoyment of different sorts of humor. I have discussed, in fact, almost everyone in the world, for everyone can respond (at least to some extent) to humorous messages. In this chapter, however, I deal with a very small group—the creators of humor. They can be divided into two categories: *professionals* and *amateurs*.

By *professionals*, I mean those who make their living from humorous composition—cartoonists, writers of comedies, satires, or skits, and so on—whose "product" is known, appreciated, and "bought" by other people. Entertainers who can present and add to material written by others also fall into this category. Some are of enduring fame: Charlie Chaplin and Woody Allen in the cinema; Norman Lear (the spiritual father of Archie Bunker) in television; James Thurber in literature; and Charles Addams in cartoons. As to others less famous, anyone who can make a living from humor creation is undoubtedly highly gifted.

Amateurs can make others laugh with their funny remarks and jokes, or even with skits and cartoons, but they do not regard humor as their profession. Those closest to them know how funny they are; indeed, in every meeting of a social group over a period of time, amateur humorists will emerge and be "known" for their humor. But professionals and amateurs are much more different than they are alike. What they do share is their creative ability; we know little in general about this quality, and even less about the forms it takes in humor.

THE CONCEPT OF CREATIVITY
AND ITS MEASUREMENT
IN PSYCHOLOGY

Creativity is the ability to see and present things in a new light. This fresh view finds expression in products that may be scattered over all areas of human activity, but that are generally associated with the arts and sciences. The composer working on a symphony, an author writing a novel, a mathematician building a theory — all approach their work primarily through the mind, in a kind of mental process known as *divergent thinking*. This concept was suggested by Guilford (1959), a psychologist who gave impetus to the scientific study of the process of creation by contrasting two types of thought, *convergent* and *divergent*. It is with the help of *convergent thinking* that we try to find the correct solution to a problem, for which purpose we need to know the problem's various data, to understand their logical connection, and to take the accepted way of dealing with them. For example, what is the missing number in the following series?

$$1, 2, 5, 10, \ldots, 37$$

This question has only one solution, and it can be found only when we find the rule operating in the series. Intelligence tests measure convergent thinking.

Divergent thinking, which does not strive toward a specific solution, is called for when a problem can have several equally good answers. In such a case, one plays with different ideas and possibilities and chooses the ones that seem most appropriate; convergent thinking in this situation would produce impoverished results. As an example, let us take two descriptions of a road accident, one written by a policeman and the other by a great author. They will certainly be different: The first will be a report sticking to the facts and using convergent thinking to do it properly, while the second will be free to make its choice among many ideas in order best to convey to the reader the *feeling* of the accident. An author, that is to say, thinks divergently.

In the last 20 years, psychological research has concentrated on several aspects of divergent thinking. Special tests, called *creativity tests,* have been constructed (Getzels & Jackson, 1962; Taylor & Baron,

1963; Torrance, 1974). They measure the following aspects of divergent thinking: *fluency, flexibility, elaboration,* and *originality.* Let us take an example from one question used in such tests: "What are the possible uses of a cardboard box?" People are encouraged to give as many answers to such a question as they can, and the variables of divergent thinking are scored and quantified on the basis of these answers, as follows:

> *Fluency* is scored by the number of answers given. Thus, the richness of thought is quantified.
>
> *Flexibility* means the number of times that the focus of thought moves from one area to another. Take the following answers to the question given above: "To hold buttons," "To collect coins in," "To keep paper clips in," "Make it into a hat," and "Make it into a doll's hat." The score here is 2, because the first three answers deal with the box as a container, and then the focus of thought shifts to the idea of the box as a hat.
>
> *Elaboration* means the number of times the respondent adds an extra element to the stimulus (the cardboard box) in order to give a fresh answer—for example, "Fill a box with earth and grow flowers in it."
>
> *Originality* is scored by counting the answers that are only rarely given but are appropriate.

The addition of the four scores on these variables makes for a subject's creativity score. Example 11.1 lists the answers given by two adolescents to the "box" question on a creativity test, and compares their scores.

Many research projects have been focused on finding differences between persons who are high and low in creativity. In studies in which the humor variable has been introduced, it has clearly been shown that those high in creativity are (as a group) more open to humor than those low in creativity. Correlations between humor and creativity are positive and statistically significant (O'Connell, 1969; Rouff, 1975; Ziv, 1981). In the next chapter, I show how humor can be quantified.

Why is humor related to creativity? It seems that these two concepts have a common core. Arthur Koestler, in his brilliant *The Act*

EXAMPLE 11.1
Creativity in a Cardboard Box

In a study of creativity (Ziv, 1980), 16-year-olds of both sexes were asked, "What can be done with a cardboard box?" These were David's and Sara's answers:

David	Sara
Put papers in it	Put things in it
Put flowers in it	A base for a table lamp
Put buttons in it	A baby's cot
Keep books in it	An ashtray for heavy smokers
A drawer	A rain hat
Put food in it	Use for making a bonfire
A toy for a child	Use for basketball practice
A doll's house	Make into a picture with gouache paints
Serve food in it	Upside down—a chair for a very thin kid
Dog kennel	For sailing on a pond for a few seconds
Draw on it	Garbage pail
Make two holes for a mask	Topographical map with projections and depressions
Base for a tree	Niche for a statue
Waste paper basket	A safe—for a country of honest people
Teach geometry	To hide the TV screen when programs are bad
Burn it	To keep lists of promises of political candidates before elections (you need a huge box)
Painting box	To keep lists of fulfilled promises of the same people (you need a very small box)

As can be seen, although Sara and David gave the same number of answers, there are qualitative differences between their lists. Sara has higher scores on flexibility, elaboration, and originality; thus, on the basis of this test, she can be considered more creative than David.

133

of Creation (1964), introduced the idea that understanding humor is the best way to the comprehension of scientific discovery and artistic creativity. The common factor in humor, art, and science is the concept of *bisociation,* which is illustrated in Figures 5.2 and 5.3 (see Chapter 5). Mark Twain was certainly very much aware of humor as a form of bisociation. He wrote that "wit is the sudden marriage of ideas which before their union were not perceived to have any relation" (Clemens, 1935, p. 185).

Creative people have the ability to look beyond the obvious, to see relationships in unusual and new ways, and to be open and flexible. They are not prisoners of habitual ways of thinking. They can use novel approaches, and "local logic" is quite acceptable to them in the appropriate frame of reference. Therefore, their intellectual processes are open to humor.

Creative thinking can be found among people in many different professions. Why do some highly creative people choose science, others art, and still others humor as a profession? In this chapter and the next, I describe those blessed with the power of divergent thought who choose to express their talents through humor. How do they differ from other creative persons? What are the characteristics of the humorist's personality?

First, however, I must emphasize that creativity demands not only a certain kind of thinking, but also, and as importantly, the ability to translate ideas into a given medium such as writing or drawing. Nor is that all; strenuous effort and perseverance are also essential. Herein lies the difference between the professional and the amateur in any field, including humor. The amateur who invents a joke in ordinary social interaction is "translating" his specific kind of thinking into a spontaneous form that he himself broadcasts to others. But the professional works hard and steadily at realizing his ideas and using all his abilities, and then passes his product to agents who present it to the public. A comic playwright hands over his play to a producer and actors, and they become his intermediaries with the public. Writers of humorous columns and cartoonists similarly use newspapers as their agent for reaching a wide audience. A professional has a work schedule and commitments as to time and even quantity of work, and he has no direct connection with his public. The amateur has much more freedom, and can spontaneously create humor directed at a specific group that is known to him personally.

The remainder of this chapter examines the personality of the professional humorist.

THE PROFESSIONAL HUMORIST

Historically, the professional humorist has had an important role, which has generally been social in its nature. The comedy and satire of ancient Greece presented society with a humorously distorted image of itself. The audience often laughed at its leaders and sometimes, unawares, at itself. In primitive societies the humorist had a privileged position as the one person allowed to laugh at everything, however sacred. His later cousin, the court jester, played a similar role for kings and nobles.

The court jester was at the same time the creator and the performer of humor. Later, specialization came into this field, as into many others. Today we have two distinct varieties of professional humorists: writers and performers. To the writers we should add those who create humor in other media, such as cartoonists, for instance. We should also remember that some writers of humorous material also perform it themselves, but in most cases this is not so. There is no doubt that those who write are more creative than those who perform; in our contemporary framework, however, the performers generally are better known (and better paid) than the people who create their material. This can easily be understood, because the performers are the ones who face the public, who are applauded or booed, and — the most important factor in the field of humor — who get the laughs.

Research focusing on humor as a profession is only a recent phenomenon, and data is very scanty; the unknown greatly outweighs the known. There are three main sources of scientific information: biographical studies, interviews, and psychological tests. The first category includes autobiogaphies, such as Charlie Chaplin's (1966); biographies, such as Lax's book on Woody Allen (1975); and a few books that analyze the lives of humorists, such as Pannenbourg's *Les Écrivains Satiriques (The Satirists)* (1954).

Systematic interviews with professional humorists are recent additions to the field. It should be stressed that systematic interviews are rather different from journalistic ones in their scope, their methodology, and the hypotheses generated. Fry and Allen's book *Make 'Em Laugh* (1975) and Janus's study of professional comedians (1975) are instances of this kind of work. There is one methodological point I would like to make in connection with studies based on interviews. In general, scientific studies guard the anonymity of the persons interviewed. This is important not only for the subjects themselves, but also for the author of such a study. If he gives their real names, he is generally rather favorable in his descriptions, since otherwise he may be attacked for libelous distortion. He is also under some tacit obligation toward his subjects, who, let us not forget, have voluntarily cooperated with him. This might explain in part why the humorists described by Fry and Allen* appear in a much more positive light than those interviewed by Janus, who preserved the anonymity of his subjects. Of course it is possible, but not very probable, that the latter actually did have more negative traits than the former; in any case, one has to be careful of the methodological dangers involved in naming names.

The third source we have on professional humorists consists of studies in which psychological tests were administered. Apart from my own research with Israeli humorists, only Janus (1975) and Fisher and Fisher (1982), to my knowledge, have used such an approach. Janus reported results from intelligence tests, and the Fishers used results from projective techniques. In my own research, I used tests and questionnaires, and measured the personality dimensions described in Chapter 9.

From all this material, we can get a general picture of the background and personality characteristics of professional humorists. This is not by any means to imply that they are all alike; each has his own individuality. But some aspects of personality frequently found among them may help us to understand them as a professional group. I attempt here to synthesize all that is known at present about professional humorists from the different sources mentioned above. Since there is very little material about writers as such, it is not possible to differentiate them from performers, and so I consider them as a single group. When important characteristics of one professional category appear vis-à-vis the other, I point them out.

*They are all well known in America today: Norman Lear, Jack Elinson, Ruth Flippen, Billy Barnes, Herby Baker, Arnie Rosen, and Bob Henry.

Although there are some discrepancies among research results, a general and tentative picture of professional humorists does emerge. I organize the material under three main headings:

1. Family background and education.
2. Ideas about humor.
3. Personality.

The discussion of family background and education may help us to understand some circumstances that may be seen as preconditions for humor development. The discussion of ideas about humor is intended to clarify conceptual views on humor from the viewpoint of those who produce and present it. The examination of humorists' personalities is divided on the lines of the personality model defined in Chapter 9: Intellectual factors, sociability, and emotionality are examined.

However, one word of caution is in order: Most research results at present are based on male humorists. Especially among writers and cartoonists, there are very few professional female humorists. (The question of sex differences is taken up in the next chapter, when amateur humorists are discussed.) Consequently, it must be borne in mind that these descriptions relate mostly to men; a group of female humorists might present a different picture, but no one really knows for certain.

Family Background and Education

Most of the humorists investigated, both in the United States and in Israel, originally came from relatively low-income groups; their families ranked as members of the lower middle class. Most also belong to minority groups, with a high preponderance of Jews in the American sample.

Family life was generally full of conflicts between parents. Many humorists have located the roots of their humor in this atmosphere. Norman Lear described the unending battle between his parents: "I came from a family who yelled a great deal. They lived at the top of their lungs always. The only defense against that was to laugh at it, find what was funny in it" (Fry & Allen, 1975, p. 21).

"The continual fight between my parents was hell. It frightened me, I wanted to run away, I didn't know what to do. I believe that I became the classroom clown as a defense — others enjoyed what I was doing for a change," one performer told me, visibly still hurt by what had happened between his parents. Talking about her experience as a child performer, Ruth Flippen compared the applause she got on stage with the love and approval she needed from her parents.

In an interview published in *McCall's* (Meryman, 1978), Carol Burnett told of her miserable childhood with two alcoholic parents who were always fighting. It is interesting to note that when Goertzel and Goertzel (1962) analyzed the biographies of 300 famous people of the 20th century, 24 of them had alcoholic parents; 11 of these became well-known humorists, Bernard Shaw among them. A child can be broken by such a household, but he may also deny its misery by turning it into something funny and so making it easier to handle. Describing his difficult childhood, Art Buchwald (1967) stressed the value of laughter in becoming accepted. When he asked Abbott ("the fat one" in the Abbott-Costello team) what makes a person creative, Abbott replied without hesitation, "A difficult childhood."

Most of the humorists examined had closer and warmer relations with their mothers and poorer ones with their fathers, who were generally weak figures in the household. In many cases the mothers contributed to their children's success through a pushiness that was sometimes expressed in blackmail: "You can do exactly what you want, but if you don't go on in your marvelous way which will certainly take you to success, you'll break my heart." The Israeli humorist who thus described his mother's help added, "But I guess that most Jewish mothers are like that." This remark may remind one of what Dan Greenberg wrote in his famous book, *How to Be a Jewish Mother* (1965): "You don't have to be Jewish in order to be a Jewish mother." Does this family pattern explain why so many humorists in America are Jewish? Probably not, since in Israel most mothers are Jewish and the number of humorists is sadly small.

In spite of the fact that the mothers of most humorists were the dominant figures in their childhoods, the fathers were perceived as having more humor. One exception to the findings concerning the relations with parents is the Fisher and Fisher study (1982). They interviewed and tested 43 comedians and compared them with a group of 41 actors. As opposed to the actors, the comics were found to have had better relations with their fathers, while their mothers were criti-

cal and demanding. It is possible that actors have even worse relations with their fathers than comedians (this, of course, does not necessarily mean that comedians have good ones). Goertzel and Goertzel
(1962) reported that all famous actors in their sample came from
troubled homes. This is certainly not so for all the professional humorists investigated here; despite the atmosphere of conflict in the families of most humorists, humor and laughter were frequently present
as well. Many talked about humorous models for imitation — a parent
with a healthy sense of humor, a grandparent with whom a child could
identify.

The overall picture of the typical humorist's background, despite
mitigating factors, is a gloomy one — a poor family struggling for sub-
sistence in an atmosphere of parental conflict. The humor that develops
in such a situation is both a defense mechanism and a means of coping with difficulties; it attacks and distorts reality, makes it funny, and
therefore makes it tolerable. Of course, an unhappy childhood will
not produce a humorist if the talent is lacking.

As for educational background, most of the humorists had rather
unfavorable memories of school. They were critical about how the educational system is organized, and many had very low opinions of their
teachers. One humorist in my sample said, "My teachers weren't really
interested in kids. They just came, talked, bored us, and never tried
to understand us or ask what we were interested in." Another, a famous
satirist, said that teachers were his first victims: "Making fun of them,
ridiculing, and laughing at them was a real vengeance for me and a
real threat for the other kids. I guess I should be grateful to my teachers — they supplied me with ideal targets for training in satire." With
very few exceptions, all the humorists stated that school was a great
disappointment, that they were unable to make meaningful contact
with their teachers, and that their studies bored them. Mark Twain
spoke for many when he wrote, "In the first place, God made idiots.
This was for practice. Then he made School Boards" (Clemens, 1935,
p. 76).

It is fascinating and, from the educational establishment's point
of view, rather sad that some brilliant humorists did not finish high
school and have a low opinion of formal schooling. Humorists are highly intelligent people, but most of them were patent failures in school.
Low grades, feelings of alienation, and a desire to escape are very much
alive in their schoolday memories. On the other hand, all have read

widely, and many describe themselves as autodidacts. I was astonished
to find in some humorists with a very poor level of formal education
a wealth of cultural knowledge in various fields. One of the studies
of Woody Allen and his comedy (Lax, 1975) describes his unsuccess-
ful efforts to get settled in college, though so great was his intellectual thirst that he procured private tutors and with their help studied
philosophy, literature, and other subjects.

The formal educational level attained by the writers was higher
than that of the performers, but they expressed the same disappointment in regard to school.

Ideas about Humor

Philosophers and psychologists who try to understand humor and propose different theories, without being able to arrive at a consensus,
should find some solace in the fact that humorists are no nearer a consensus themselves. Those humorists who are willing to explain what
humor is — and many are not even prepared to try — have many and
varied views.

For some, humor is an inborn trait, and therefore it requires no
explanations. For others, it is simply the use of certain techniques.
One humorist in my sample said that what is important is the motivation to make people laugh: "If this is what you really want, you can
learn techniques how to do it — anybody can learn it." However, as
common sense would have it, most believe that humor is in part an
inborn talent, but that it can be improved by learning and modeling.

For some, all humor is aggressive, and a joke is always at someone's expense: "Without a victim, there's no fun; people love to see how
ridiculous others are. Maybe this is a way of saying that others are
not only awful, but by comparison, I'm not so bad." Many agree that
humor can be a rather devastating weapon. One of the satirists in my
sample said,

> You can fight back even against those who have enormous power. Pol-
> iticians who make our lives miserable, who can send us to war and use
> pretentious and overinflated patriotic arguments, can be shown as ridic-
> ulous human beings. Laughter at them can be like a pin deflating a
> balloon — it is big and seems impressive, but in reality it is full of . . .
> air.

At the opposite extreme, we find humorists who believe that humor is an expression of love:

> Tell people about your worries and troubles and they'll find a reflection of their own worries and troubles. Show them that you, and therefore they, can laugh at all that. You create a real community for a while, a fraternity based on understanding and love.

One comedian said that all he is doing is to bring people together for shared pleasure: "Sometimes I believe that I'm a real benefactor — I should be canonized."

Changing people's mood — making them happier for a short time — seems to be a crucial motivation for humor, from the point of view of many performers. In the Fishers' sample, this theme appears frequently. "I love people and I want to show them my love," said one; another said, "I love everybody." In my own sample, a famous comedian described his role in time of war. In Israel, most comedians are mobilized during wars to tour the battlefields, improvising and presenting shows that boost the troops' morale. This man told me that he had arrived at one unit just after a fierce battle in which many soldiers had died. Contrary to what usually happens when he arrives — everybody comes joyously to relax for a while — on this occasion nobody was interested. The unit's commander decided to cancel the show. The comedian, with tears in his eyes, pleaded with the commander to let him begin, even if only a handful of soldiers were to appear. Finally the commander agreed, and a few soldiers showed up. The comedian started carefully and slowly.

> I somehow made them giggle. Then they started laughing and their laughter was like a bell. Others came and in the end we were laughing and singing together. I thanked God that he had given me the power to be able to make them forget for a few seconds; to change their tears into smiles.

One important difference between writers and performers emerged in my interviews. While most writers saw in humor a way of coping with their own difficulties and life's miseries and of influencing others, most performers accentuated humor's role as a way of getting attention and acceptance. Many writers described humor as a defense mech-

anism against their disappointments and frustrations in childhood or
adolescence. One said, "If someone is too fond of humor, you don't
have to look too deeply to find in the background a lot of personal misery." Another, a virulent satirist, said,

> For me humor is clearly a sublimation for aggression. When I was a
> kid I was physically aggressive, getting easily into fistfights. Slowly I
> discovered that humor can be more efficient; the more I used humor
> against others, the less did I need physical violence. For me humor was,
> and is, therapeutic. I believe that for most people it must have a simi-
> lar function.

This brings me to a special word about satirists. The professional
literature does not deal kindly with them. Drawing on biographies,
Pannenbourg (1954) compared satirists with humorists in his book on
satirical writers. Byron, Gogol, Heine, Swift, Rabelais, and Voltaire
were among the satirists he studied. Describing their characters, he
wrote: "They were egotistic, immoral, and ambitious, and lacked genuine feelings for others, including their families and children; they were
hypocrites, loners, and self-admirers" (p. 193; translation mine). In
his book on the sense of humor, Bergler (1956), drawing on personal
impressions, says, "Satirists seem to be on the borderline of psychotic
depression; their saving grace is an occasional manic defense" (p. 164).
These are harsh words. In my interviews with satirists I did find some
of these characteristics, but I also found them to have a genuine interest in what is going on around them. They are socially minded;
they want to improve society; and they desperately seek understanding and acceptance. For most of them satire is a way of dealing with
authority, which is perceived as frightening. While fighting it, however, they seek the sympathy of the underdog, and as one of them said,
"The majority of people are underdogs."

As for performers, their main motivation seems to be related to
a striving for acceptance and love. This stems from the same roots
of insecurity and disappointment as the writers' needs, but because
of their different talents, and possibly because of their strong exhibi-
tionistic urges, they choose performance as their mode. One extremely
talented comedian told us that all actors, tragic or comic, share a similar hunger for attention:

We always want to be on stage, to put on costumes, to be different persons and characters and to be admired. My belief is that comics need
more acceptance than other actors. We don't want to be hated even if
it's only in a play; we want to be constantly liked and to be associated
with joy and laughter, never with gloom or tears.

This rich insight into comedians' motivations provides an interesting
hypothesis that is well worth investigating.

Personality

Professional humorists have rather complex personalities. The description that follows is a fairly general one, and although it more or less
fits most of those studied, there are many exceptions. It should be re-
called that the scientific study of professional humorists is only beginning, and that new findings will probably challenge today's scanty
knowledge. However, three relatively large samples are available from
psychological research:

1. Janus (1975) studied 55 professional stand-up comedians.
2. Fisher and Fisher (1982) tested and interviewed 43 comedians
and clowns.
3. I myself worked with 21 humorists—nine writers and 12 performers.

This total of 119 professional humorists might not seem very im-
pressive. However, let us not forget that humorists belong to a fairly
rare species. Compared to other professional writers (the so-called "serious" ones) and performers, humorists are a very small minority. We
must hope that more research will come to enrich our knowledge about
these wonderful people who contribute to make our lives (at least briefly) more pleasurable.

I use the personality model outlined in Chapter 9, looking first
at the intellectual dimension, then at the social dimension, and finally at the emotional dimension.

Let us recall that there is a hierarchy of the three dimensions.
When we discussed humor enjoyment, we talked about the social dimension first, because it is the most important element in humor en-

joyment (see pp. 126–127). In humor creation, the most important dimension is the cognitive one, followed by the social dimension, and then by the emotional one. Let us start, therefore, by looking into the intellectual dimension of humor creation.

Intelligence. Professional humorists are highly intelligent. In his work with professional comedians, Janus (1975) administered one sub-test of the Wechsler Adult Intelligence Scale and found that IQs ranged from 115 to 160 + (although he writes that three comedians in the sample scored between 108 and 115; see p. 170). The mean score of the sample was 138, which places the group in the highest 2% of the population. But Janus used only the vocabulary subtest of the Wechsler Adult Intelligence Scale, which measures verbal ability alone. It should not be surprising that professional stand-up comedians should have extremely high scores on such a test. In their profession they have to rely mostly upon verbal ability, and it is also possible that their verbal mastery was one of the reasons for their choice of profession in the first place.

In addition let us not forget that these were very successful people, nationally known, who had been in the comedy field for at least 10 years and were mostly earning salaries of six figures or over. It is probable that a sample of the people who have succeeded in any profession will constitute a highly intelligent group. This is certainly true for any profession in which considerable verbal ability is necessary.

In my own sample, I found that writers as a group were more intelligent than performers. The main scores on intelligence tests for the two groups were 132.4 for writers and 118.3 for performers. Instead of applying only a verbal subtest, as Janus did, I used one of the best-known nonverbal general intelligence tests — the Raven matrices. This test is widely employed in Israel, and up-to-date norms are available.

The use of a nonverbal general intelligence test instead of a verbal one probably explains why the humorists in my sample had lower scores than those reported in Janus's study. But even with this test, professional humorists emerged as highly intelligent. They had a mean IQ of 125.7, which places them in the highest 3.5% of the population. We must remember that such a level of intelligence is probably to be found in any group of successful professionals. As Chapter 12 indicates, high intelligence — contrary to what might be expected — is not one of the main characteristics of the run-of-the-mill amateur humorists.

In addition to intelligence tests, I applied some creativity tests to a few of the humorists in my sample. Their scores, calculated according to the variables mentioned at the beginning of this chapter (fluency, flexibility, elaboration, and originality), were extremely high. In particular, the scores for originality were truly spectacular. In an average test of creativity, one finds that about 3% of the total responses can be considered original; no fewer than 32% of the humorists' answers belonged to this category, however. When the creativity scores of amateur humorists are presented in Chapter 12, data on the professionals' scores are also included.

The social dimension.   I have indicated in Chapter 10 that extroverts enjoy humor more than introverts, and I have explained why this is so. The situation is rather different for professional humorists. A striking fact that one rapidly discovers when working with professional humorists is that most of them are very serious people; contrary to expectation, they do not laugh much.

Although there are significant differences between writers and performers, professional humorists as a group are more introverted than the general population. Performers have to mingle and interact with many people in their professional lives, but in private they are rather reclusive. They report having few real friends, and they prefer staying at home with their families to going to parties. They enjoy being in front of a crowd, standing on a stage, and getting all the attention, but they hate being part of a crowd. They do not use their talents as humorists much in social gatherings. One of them told me that one of his most hated moments (and he has many of them) is when somebody in a group asks him, "with a stupid smile on his face," to tell a joke. For some, such social expectations are given as reasons for staying away from company. A brilliant performer described his profound need to be accepted while on stage and left alone in his private life in the following way:

> I'm not very easygoing in my private life; I find it difficult to make small talk, and actually I prefer to be alone or with my wife to going out and meeting people. When I have to, I'm ill at ease and wish the whole thing were over. On stage, I'm sure of myself; I know that they've come — and paid — to listen to me. For a short moment, I'm the most interesting person around. I like it, and I wonder if my joy in the profession is not related to my desire to be the best.

Writers are even more introverted than performers. As one of the writers in my sample explained,

> Writing humor, like any other thing, is a lonely activity. If you want to create, you have to work on it. You are turning ideas in your head, writing and throwing a lot into the wastebasket, rewriting, polishing — and all this cannot be done with others around you.

He added, "You need people because they are your material — you have to watch them, understand them, and even guess what will amuse them. But [you don't have] to be absorbed and preoccupied with them."

Summarizing his findings about stand-up comedians, Janus wrote, "For the most part, comedians are shy, sensitive, fearful individuals" (1975, p. 174). Woody Allen is an archetype of introversion such as Jung might have dreamed of. As a child, Allen tried to learn magic tricks in order to become popular. About this period, he has said, "Magic fit into everything I needed at the time. It kept me isolated from the world. It was so much better than school, which was boring, frightening" (Lax, 1975, p. 30).

When I tested professional humorists, I found that their scores on extroversion were significantly lower than the control group's. As the data on test results presented in Chapter 12 indicate, professional humorists are more introverted than amateurs. However, a few performers are, on the contrary, extremely extroverted. These seem to be unable to stop cracking jokes and make every possible effort to be at the center of any social gathering. But they are more the exception than the rule; I have more to say later about the intriguing phenomenon of the compulsive humorist.

There is one interesting point related to the social dimension of the personality of professional humorists: their desire to feel that they have power over others. Writers, particularly satirists, want to make people act and take up a position in the struggle against the existing political power. But even performers seem fascinated by power; the feeling that they can manipulate their public is appealing to them. In the words of one of them, "It's fantastic to feel the public in your power. They laugh when I want [them to] and they don't laugh when I don't [want] them to. It's exhilarating." It might be that this preoccupation with power is related to the feelings of powerlessness that professional humorists experience in the emotional dimension of their personalities.

The emotional dimension.   As a group, professional humorists are highly emotional. The existing studies, in general, support the old stereotype of the sad clown. The stand-up comedians in Janus's sample spoke of anxiety and sometimes of depression; humor, for them, was a means of active confrontation with these feelings. Janus writes that "life always seemed to the comics to present situations in which they were misunderstood and picked on or belittled" (1975, p. 171).

Feelings of inferiority and worthlessness were predominant in the projective tests administered by Fisher and Fisher (1982) to their sample of comedians, who felt depreciated, unworthy, and preoccupied with their acceptance by others. They tended to work very hard to convince others (and probably themselves even more) that they love people and that the world is not as bad as it seems.

Of Janus's sample, 80% had been in some kind of psychotherapy. The reason most often given for seeking professional help was "a pervasive feeling of depression." However, few stayed in therapy for long; relationships with their therapists were tainted by a power struggle. The comedians tried to manipulate the people offering help into a position of inferiority by inviting them to their shows, in the discussion of which they became the experts themselves. This is another example of their efforts to compensate for their feelings of inferiority. Even while asking for help, they were afraid that psychotherapy might diminish their ability to make others laugh. It looks as though comedians feel unconsciously that humor stems from suffering; if they cease to suffer, they might cease to be successful.

Janus (1975) writes that several subjects in his sample related the joke about the comedian who went into analysis:

He told me to lie down on the couch and tell him everything I know.
And now he's doing my act in Philadelphia.

Their success seemed to them only temporary, and they were constantly afraid of falling into oblivion.

In my sample, only 20% of the professional humorists were in therapy. Compared to the 80% in Janus's sample, it would seem that the Israelis needed less psychological help than their American peers. But this is probably more a cultural difference than anything else. How many successful people in the performing arts, "earning salaries of six figures or more," have been in some kind of psychotherapy in Amer-

---

EXAMPLE 11.2
Tentative Generalizations about Professional Humorists

The great majority of professional humorists are men.

Most of them come from lower-middle-class families.

Most experienced parental conflict at home.

Their mothers were understanding and encouraging, even unduly so.

In most families, they had a model for humor and laughter.

Their level of formal education is rather low, and school was hated. However, many are successful autodidacts with a wide range of knowledge.

Personal difficulties constituted part of their motivation for choosing humor as a profession. Humor is seen as an efficient way of coping with anxiety—a defense mechanism.

They are highly intelligent (especially on verbal tests) and very creative.

Socially, they are rather introverted; writers are more introverted than performers.

There is a hidden desire for power and domination in most of them.

They are highly emotional and are less stable than the general population.

Negative self-images, anxiety, and insecurity appear rather frequently.

---

ica? My guess would be that the percentage is not significantly different from the one reported on comedians. In Israel, psychotherapy is not as widely resorted to as in the United States. In addition, no humorist in Israel (and probably no writer or actor) earns a salary of the size common in America.

Feelings of anxiety, inferiority, and unhappiness appeared less frequently in the interviews with professional Israeli humorists, as compared with the Americans. However, their test results showed that they were less stable and more emotional than the general population. They were less happy, less sure of themselves, and emotionally more fragile than the controls. In spite of their success in their profession, their self-image was more negative than the self-images of others.

To sum up what we know from psychological research about the personalities of professional humorists, I should like to stress again that they are not a homogeneous group—far from it, in fact. However, some generalizations can be made from the existing studies. These are summarized in Example 11.2.

Let us now turn to those who use humor in everyday life, but who are not professional humorists.

12

The Humorists among Us:
The Amateurs

Humor blossoms mainly among friends. Most of it is spontaneous, produced on the spur of the moment and relating to the here and now of social interaction. A study published in 1976 compared reasons for laughter as reported by students in 1937 and 1973 (Pollio & Edgerly, 1976). First, it was found that the average student laughs on the average 15–20 times a day. Second, the main reasons for laughter had not changed much in 35 years. Formal funny materials (plays, movies, etc.) accounted for only 20% of the laughter that was occasioned.

We make one another laugh — sometimes involuntarily, but mostly on purpose. Some of us are more adept than others at provoking laughter, and some enjoy a greater number of humorous situations and enjoy them more fully than others do. In this chapter, I attempt to describe the personalities of those among us who are blessed with a healthy sense of humor. To differentiate them from the professional humorists discussed in the preceding chapter, I call them "amateur" humorists.

How are humorists to be identified? With professionals, identification is relatively easy: Their productions (comedies, books, articles) are recognized as such, and those who present comic material may make millions laugh. The amateur is rarely known outside the circle of his friends or coworkers. However, he certainly contributes more to laughter within his own group than do the professional humorists, whose acting and writing are less frequently encountered. The identification of amateur humorists was the first task in my research on them (Ziv, 1979a). Once I knew who they were, they could be compared with others who had less humor, and this made it easier to grasp the nature of their personalities.

Before I describe how I detected the humorists in a group, one point has to be stressed. This book deals only with adults and adolescents, for their modes of understanding and creating humor are similar. Children of different ages, however, all enjoy kinds of humor that adults do not much appreciate. Because they are at lower levels of cognitive development, children do not always understand adult humor. Adults and adolescents have reached the stage of formal thought, and therefore share the conceptual abilities necessary for grasping forms of humor that cannot be comprehended by children. For those interested in the developmental aspects of humor, McGhee's book *Humor: Its Origins and Development* (1979) is a must.

I now explain the method I used to identify humorists.

IDENTIFYING AMATEUR HUMORISTS

It is exciting to research areas of human behavior that have been relatively untapped by the known methodological approaches. Humor is certainly one of these. My idea was to create measuring instruments that could quantify the two main dimensions of humor previously described: creativity and appreciation.

The first step was to set up a situation, as close as possible to real life, that could be observed without interfering with the subjects. I invited a group of 20 Boy and Girl Scouts, aged 16–17, to the university, and explained that my colleagues and I were doing research on group interaction and would like to ask for their cooperation. Ten psychologists sat around the room; each observed two specific subjects, as well as the group as a whole. The psychologists were graduate students, trained for the particular observations planned. Their task was to tally every instance of laughter observed for each subject, in addition to every occasion on which the subject made at least five other group members laugh (i.e., 25% of the group). *Laughter* and *smiling* were defined for the purposes of the tally, and training sessions where the graduate students scored group interactions presented on videotapes were organized. Only when satisfactory interrater reliability had been obtained did research itself start. The definitions of *smiling* and *laughter,* and the instructions that were given to the observers, are presented in Example 12.1.

As noted in Example 12.1, the quantification of each participant's

---

EXAMPLE 12.1
Operational Definitions for Observation

The following instructions were given to all observers:
A *smile* is characterized by a widening of the mouth that reveals its corners. *Laughter* is a smile plus baring of the teeth and audible sounds. These sounds accompany changes in respiration (described by Darwin in 1872 as "short and broken respirations with prolonged expirations"; (see Darwin, 1872, p. 72). Scoring is as follows:

> No response or blank face = 0
> Smile   = 1
> Laughter   = 2

Each time a subject responds with a smile, he scores 1; each time he responds with laughter, he scores 2. These responses are to be tallied in the column for humor appreciation.
Each time a subject's remark or gesture provokes at least five responses of smiling or laughter, score 1 for smiling and 2 for laughter in the column for humor creation.

---

laughter or humorous remarks was the starting point for creating two scores: one for humor appreciation and one for humor creation. Three observational measures were used for each dimension. A brief description of the situations observed follows.

Humor Creation

Creative ideas. We asked our subjects to think of possible responses to situations similar to those used in creativity tests. I give a short description of such tests at the beginning of Chapter 11; Example 11.1 shows the suggestions of two adolescents for possible uses of cardboard boxes. Tasks used in the observational situations included the following:

1. What would happen if instead of hearing and vision, scent were to become the predominant sense in humans?
2. A businessman orders 20,000 pairs of shoes from Hong Kong. On delivery, he discovers that he has received 20,000 left shoes. In the meantime, the factory in Hong Kong has gone bankrupt. What can he do?
3. What would happen if trees and flowers could walk?

Answers that provoked smiles or laughter in at least five members of the group were scored for the respondent as humorous creations.

Cartoon captions. Each subject received a booklet of 10 cartoons without captions. Subjects were encouraged to write the funniest possible captions for each of the cartoons. These were later scored for funniness by qualified judges.

Finishing jokes. Each subject received a booklet of 10 jokes with missing endings. Subjects were asked to give the funniest possible ending to each joke. Their suggestions were also scored for humorousness by qualified judges.

Humor Appreciation

Laughing while listening to humor. After pretesting, I played a record that provoked much laughter among adolescents. It had been selected by taking humorous records and an instrument measuring the amplitude and duration of the laughter aroused into different classrooms. The record that elicited the highest laughter response was then used in our observations.

Laughing at creative ideas. Laughing at creative ideas was the response of each group member to the creative ideas proposed by others.

Evaluating cartoons' funniness. Before subjects were asked to write captions for the cartoon booklet, each subject was requested to rate each cartoon for funniness on a scale from 1 ("not funny at all") to 5 ("very funny").

The intercorrelations among these six measures are presented in Table 12.1. Based on the results, two composite scores were computed: one for humor creativity and one for humor appreciation. Two additional measures were constructed: a test of the sociometry of humor and a questionnaire measuring sense of humor.

Test of the Sociometry of Humor

Tests of the sociometry of humor can be used in groups where the participants know one another well and have frequent occasions for interaction. The scouts in our group were in such a position, both in school and in their extracurricular activities.

The test I used for the sociometry of humor was presented in the following way. The names of all the students were set down on a form with four columns: "No sense of humor at all," "Not much sense of

Table 12.1
Intercorrelations among Humor Measures

Measure	Cartoon Captions	Finishing Jokes	Laughing while Listening	Laughing at Creative Ideas	Evaluating Cartoons' Funniness
Creative ideas	.34*	.29*	.21	.23	.18
Cartoon captions		.32*	.25	.21	.24
Finishing jokes			.17	.26	.38*
Laughing while listening				.28	.32*
Laughing at creative ideas					.36*
Evaluating cartoon's funniness					

*$p < .05$.

humor," "Quite a good sense of humor," and "A very good sense of humor." My colleagues and I asked all the adolescents to think of everyone they knew and write down at the top of each column the person whom the description fitted best. This was to give each individual a personal frame of reference. Then we asked them to put an X for each of their classmates in the appropriate columns, which we then graded from 1 ("No sense of humor") up to 4. This "sociometry of humor" test is illustrated in Figure 12.1.

A score was calculated for each person from the aggregate of the others' opinions; in our group of 20, the possible total scores ranged from 20 to 80. In Figure 12.1, Tom, Dick, and Harry have the highest score (4), and Bob, Carol, and Alice have the lowest (1); Figure 12.1, of course, represents the assessment of a single subject. If most of the others in the group were to answer similarly, it would appear that Tom, Dick, and Harry do indeed have the best sense of humor in the group.

Questionnaire Measuring Sense of Humor

Drawing on existing humor questionnaires in the professional literature, to which I added other items, I constructed a questionnaire to measure sense of humor. Details about its composition, validity, and reliability are given elsewhere (Ziv, 1981). It consists of 14 items; the first seven deal with humor appreciation, while the rest deal with humor creation.

	NO SENSE OF HUMOR AT ALL	NOT MUCH SENSE OF HUMOR	QUITE A GOOD SENSE OF HUMOR	A VERY GOOD SENSE OF HUMOR
	THE NEIGHBOR	UNCLE ABE	MY GEOGRAPHY TEACHER	JOE
ANDREW		X		
BETTY			X	
BOB	X			
PETER			X	
TOM				X
CAROL	X			
PAUL			X	
SIMON		X		
MARILYN		X		
DICK				X
ALICE	X			
HARRY				X
WILLIAM		X		
HELEN			X	
JENNIFER			X	

FIGURE 12.1

Some examples of items from the questionnaire are given in Chapter 9 (see p. 112). Subjects answered each question on a scale from 1 ("very rarely") to 7 ("very frequently"). The total score on the questionnaire (humor creativity plus humor appreciation) constituted the "sense of humor" score.

Intercorrelations between the major variables measured by all the tests described here were computed (Ziv, 1981). A composite score was used to identify humorists (those obtaining high scores in comparison with others in the measured population). The low scorers were —for research purposes only—considered as nonhumorists.

With this armamentarium of methods for identifying amateur humorists, I proceeded to isolate and define their main characteristics. In describing the findings here, I employ the same outline used in Chapter 11 to describe professional humorists: background, ideas about humor, and personality. However, I begin here with one important finding that I could not apply to professional humorists: sex differences.

SEX DIFFERENCES
IN SENSE OF HUMOR

As I point out in Chapter 11, women are scarce among professional humorists. From my research, it appears that among amateurs there is a division between the sexes with respect to the two main dimensions of humor: Men create it more, and women enjoy it more. On my humor questionnaire, which has been administered to thousands of subjects in many research projects in Israel, France, and Canada, it has consistently been found that scores were not significantly at variance between the sexes. However, on humor creation and appreciation, the differences have indeed been significant. The two sexes are situated in relation to the two dimensions of humor as shown in Figure 12.2.

Before I discuss these sex differences, let me stress again that these are findings related to general populations. By no means do they imply that all males are more creative in humor than all females—far from it. One only has to think of Dorothy Parker or Carol Burnett, or, even better, those ladies one knows personally who have a won-

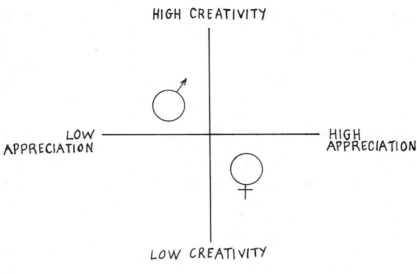

HIGH CREATIVITY

LOW
APPRECIATION

HIGH
APPRECIATION

LOW CREATIVITY

FIGURE 12.2

derful sense of humor. However, *as a group,* males score higher on the different measures for humor related to humor creativity. This has been found not only on the questionnaire measuring sense of humor, but also on the test of sociometry of humor. In addition, when they rate themselves, men give themselves higher scores than women do.

How can these sex differences be explained? First, let us note that they first appear at the end of the preschool years. This might suggest that humor is related to certain sex-role expectations (McGhee, 1979). Since (as noted in Part I) humor is most frequently either aggressive or sexual, and since the current sex-role stereotypes allot both traits more readily to men than to women, one can understand why males use more humor than females. When men are in a group by themselves (such as the army), sexual humor flourishes—often well beyond the limits of good taste. I have tried to find out if the same is true of women by themselves. In the overwhelming majority of cases, it seems that it is not. Despite the changes in the position of women brought about by the feminist movement, there is still a much stronger taboo on sexual matters among women than among men.

In developmental research, it has been found that "children who do more clowning and joking have a history of social assertiveness, including both physical and verbal aggression" (McGhee, 1979, p. 202). Since aggressiveness and dominance receive more positive reinforcement in boys than in girls, girls learn to refrain more from such forms of behavior. When my colleagues and I asked students to write down their favorite jokes, we found that males offered significantly more jokes whose functions were aggressive or sexual. Females offered more jokes with social or intellectual functions.

Another explanation, related to the question of greater female *enjoyment*, arises from the fact that emotional expression in our society is assigned to women rather than to men, and does not involve women in negative reinforcement. A little girl who comes home crying because a boy has pulled her hair will be hugged and comforted by her parents (and thus encouraged in the tearful behavior), while a boy crying for the same reason is told that "only girls cry." "Don't be a crybaby — go and hit him back." Thus expressions of feeling are more legitimate for women and come more easily to them. And just as they cry more readily, so they seem to laugh more readily. It is possible that both sexes in fact enjoy humor to the same degree, but that women are more prepared to show it by laughing. This was demonstrated in observational studies carried out by Foot and Chapman (1976). Children aged 7 and 8 were shown cartoons and unobtrusively observed. When in the company of other children, girls reciprocated boys' laughter more often than boys reciprocated girls'. In addition, boys exhibited the same amount of laughter when in the company of boys or girls. Girls, by contrast, laughed more when with boys than with girls. This finding makes one speculate about the question of the status of the sexes in our male-dominated society.

In the discussion on the social functions of humor in Chapter 3, I mention Coser's (1960) research, in which a hierarchy of humor is described: Those of higher social status use humor more often. In all hierarchical structures, those with power feel freer to use humor, and they expect their subordinates to appreciate it. Those who are low in the hierarchy know what is expected of them and pay their dues in the form of smiles or laughter. I relate in Chapter 11 the view of one of the professional humorists that making others laugh or stop laughing gives a feeling of power. It is possible that making others laugh, and laughing at the humor of others, are connected with a domination-submission relationship. As I note later on, this pattern of arousing laughter as against laughing oneself does in fact appear rather clearly in leader-follower roles.

This hypothesis — namely, that lower-status people (or, rather, those who perceive themselves as such) initiate less humor and are more ready to laugh at their own group — was verified in a research project (Nevo, 1980) in Israel. This study, drawing on findings that women laugh even more than men at jokes in which they are disparaged (Cantor, 1976; Losco & Epstein, 1975) and relating this to the lower social status of women, compared Arabs and Jews living in Israel. Jokes were constructed in which Arabs were disparaged, and others in which Jews were disparaged. As expected, Jews enjoyed the Arab-disparaging jokes more; however, the reverse was not true for the Arabs. It was found that Arabs considered jokes in which Arabs were ridiculed as funnier than those in which Jews were the victims. It is possible that the enjoyment of self-disparaging humor is a particular trait of oppressed minorities. Self-disparagement is one of the well-known characteristics of Jewish humor in the Diaspora. It serves as a defense mechanism against anxiety, as noted in Chapter 4, and it might well fulfill the same function with women. Levine (1976) showed from an analysis of male and female humorists' recordings that males' scripts contained only 12% self-disparaging remarks, while females' scripts contained 63%.

Another possible explanation for sex differences may be related to another set of social expectations. A "ladylike" appearance does not go well with the facial grimaces or bodily contortions that are frequently used to get a laugh. The circus clown is a classic example. Most comic performers are far from being handsome; some even adopt grotesque bodily postures or ridiculous paraphernalia. (Remember Groucho Marx's way of walking? His brows, mustache, and cigar?) A woman "must" seem pretty and graceful, and would be more likely to repel people than amuse them by looking weird.

I have tried to clarify how amateur humorists of both sexes see themselves. My hypothesis, based on the ideas and findings just outlined, was that female humorists would have a self-image closer to the male stereotype, in contrast with their nonhumorist peers, who would see themselves as conforming more to the female stereotype.

In order to compare amateur humorists with their nonhumorist peers, I administered three humor measurements to 344 adolescents: the test of sociometry of humor, the questionnaire measuring sense of humor, and a humor creativity test. A total humor score was computed for each subject on the aggregate of his scores. I then divided the entire research population into humorists (those with scores above

the median) and nonhumorists (the others). In addition, I administered to the entire group a self-image questionnaire, which is briefly
presented in Example 12.2.

Comparing humorists with nonhumorists, I found that humorist boys were not significantly different from their nonhumorist peers
(the only exception was on the "sociability" cluster, where humorists
scored higher). Humorist girls, however, were significantly different
from other girls: They had a more positive self-image, and they saw
themselves as having more characteristics of the male stereotype (i.e.,
they scored higher on the "machismo" cluster).

EXAMPLE 12.2
A Self-Image Questionnaire

Sixteen bipolar adjectives were presented on 10-point scales, as in
the following examples:

Active_·__·__·__·__·__·__·__·__·_·Passive
Dominant__·__·__·__·__·__·__·__·__·Submissive

The subjects were asked to put an X at the appropriate point on each scale,
according to the way they saw themselves. The scales were then scored
according to social desirability. On the first scale above, 1 point was allot-
ted to the "passive" end and 10 to the "active" end. On the second, the
highest score was assigned to the middle of the scale and the lowest ones
to the extremes.

Four clusters of scales were obtained by means of statistical analysis
(for details, see Ziv, 1981).

Flexibility: flexible, dominant-submissive, tough-soft, and stubborn-
compliant (for the last three scales, the highest scores go to the middle of the continuum).

Machismo (the higher ends of the scales only are given): self-confi-
dent, strong, courageous, quick.

Sociability (higher ends of scales only): sociable, sense of humor, active, not shy.

Optimism (higher ends of scales only): optimistic, good, orderly,
cheerful.

A total "self-concept" score was obtained by adding up the values for
each scale.

It seems, then, that humorist girls are less conformist; they reject traditional sex roles, and they dare to behave more in accordance with male than with female stereotypes. Humorist girls may find in adolescence that they do not easily win social acceptance from boys when they exhibit unfeminine traits, and it is possible that some of them learn their sense of humor in consequence. If this is so, it is regrettable for society as a whole. Since we have empirical evidence that humor can be encouraged in educational settings (Ziv, 1981), a special effort to reward the expression of humor in girls at school could contribute to diminishing some aspects of sex stereotyping.

Let us now look at the amateur humorist, following the outline used in Chapter 11 for the professional humorist.

THE AMATEUR HUMORIST

Family Background and Relationships

As opposed to professional humorists, who come mostly from middle-class and lower-class socioeconomic backgrounds, amateurs are found as frequently as nonhumorists in every socioeconomic group. In almost every group of people, at least one humorist can be found. As noted in Chapter 3, the person who makes the group laugh fulfills an important role. Amateur humorists are therefore to be found wherever durable group interactions exist.

Adult amateur humorists in my research (Ziv, 1981) were identified by means of a slightly different methodology from the one used with adolescents. In each seminar on the psychology of humor that I conducted in Israel, France, and Canada, I asked each of the participants to nominate from among his friends present two or three persons whom he considered to have a good sense of humor. I also asked each participant to name two or three people present who lacked a sense of humor. To all persons from these two groups, I administered humor tests. The results demonstrated that peer nominations are effective in identifying humorists for research purposes. As a group, humorists identified as such had significantly higher scores than nonhumorists on humor tests.

Are there any particular family relationship patterns for amateur humorists? Are they similar to those observed for professionals? In

interviews with adults, I have tried to establish the atmosphere in their
homes and the nature of their relationships with their mothers, fathers,
and other family members. Humorists and nonhumorists were indi-
vidually interviewed and tested. I found that male humorists had better
relationships with their mothers than with their fathers; this finding
is similar to that reported for professionals. However, for women, the
situation was reversed: Most of them reported better relationships with
their fathers than with their mothers. I attempt to explain these findings after I have outlined the results on the same question for adolescents.

Family relationships of adolescent humorists were studied (Ziv,
1981) using Schaeffer's (1965) parent perception questionnaire. This
has been adapted for Israeli adolescents (Klingman, 1978), and I used
it to measure humorists' and nonhumorists' perceptions of parental
acceptance. In contrast to most tests measuring child-rearing prac-
tices, Schaeffer's questionnaire does not ask parents how they behave.
Instead, children are asked to relate how they perceive their parents'
attitudes and behavior toward them. For a brief description of the
Schaeffer procedure as I used it, see Example 12.3.

This questionnaire was administered to adolescents. In the light
of their scores, I divided them into two groups: those reporting high
parental acceptance, and those reporting low acceptance. In addition,
all of the subjects underwent a battery of humor tests, and a total score
on humor was computed for each subject. Comparisons between boys
and girls reporting high and low acceptance by fathers and mothers
were made. The results of these tests indicated the following:

1. Fathers' acceptance is more important for girls. Girls who perceive their fathers as highly accepting have a better sense of humor
than boys; they also have significantly higher scores on humor than
girls reporting low acceptance by fathers. Fathers' acceptance is not
reflected in the humor scores for boys.

2. Mothers' acceptance is important to both sexes. For boys, however, it plays a more important role; this acceptance significantly differentiates between humorist scores for them, but not for girls. Mothers' acceptance is as important for humorist as for nonhumorist girls.

Possible explanations for these findings are tentative. Further research is certainly needed to clarify parental influences in the development of humor in boys and girls. However, I can propose some hy-

---

EXAMPLE 12.3
Perceiving Parental Behavior and Attitudes

A list of parental behaviors is presented to adolescents. For each statement, a response can be noted in one of three columns: "not at all like him," "somewhat like him," or "very much like him." The respondent thinks about his father and makes a note in the appropriate column for each statement. Some sample statements include the following:

He tries to relate to me as an equal.

He makes me feel at ease when I'm with him.

He tries to cheer me up when I'm sad.

He almost never takes me out with him.

He behaves as if I'm bothering him.

He doesn't know what I need or what I want.

The first three statements concern acceptance; the last three relate to rejection. Each subject is then asked to answer a second identical questionnaire concerning his mother (in which the statements of course feature "she" and "her"). The advantage of the questionnaire is that it relates to parental behaviors as they are perceived by the child. The measuring of reality is for each of us a function of what and how we perceive it.

Scores for parental acceptance are computed for mothers and fathers separately, by subtracting "rejection" from "acceptance." This is done because rejection and acceptance are the extremes of one additudinal continuum.

---

potheses. Boys who display humorous behavior act like their fathers and therefore earn their mothers' laughter, and this contributes to their acceptance by the mothers. Girls are not supposed to be funny, and mothers (as humor enjoyers rather than humor creators) do not encourage them in this form of behavior. As models for their daughters, mothers reinforce their "female" characteristics, and humor is not one of these. Fathers do not care as much as mothers about appropriately girlish behavior. When they find humor in their daughters they are proud and pleased, because, as humorists, they see themselves reflected. They value it even more, since in general they do not often encounter humor in the other sex. It is therefore possible that they reinforce this characteristic in their daughters, encouraging by their acceptance the continuation of their humorous behavior. I am now involved in research planned to verify these hypotheses.

To sum up what we know about amateur humorists' relations with their families, we can say that parental acceptance seems to be important for humor development. Mothers' acceptance seems to be more significant for boys, and fathers' acceptance for girls.

Ideas about Humor

In my research, adult amateur humorists were also compared with nonhumorists on their ideas about humor. It seems that the humorists' views on humor come closer to the ones expressed by professional performers than to those expressed by writers. While humorist writers want to influence people and teach them something, amateur humorists principally want to create a pleasurable atmosphere. The social function of humor in direct group interaction is the amateur humorist's main interest, and his main objective (though not the only one) is to be liked and accepted by others. Amateur humorists enjoy the central status humor gives them in a group, but they are also aware that sometimes they are liked and feared at the same time. One amateur humorist told me,

> They love it when I'm making fun of someone, but I wonder if secretly they aren't afraid that their turn may come, and this frightens them. In order to avoid this danger, some people try to be in my good graces, and unwillingly they attribute to me social power. And I can't honestly say that I don't enjoy it.

Many amateur humorists, mostly men, are aware that they have power in the group. Women who feel this power are careful not to endanger their ladylike image. As one woman told me,

> Nobody likes to be a target of humorous attacks. But this is especially true when a man is attacked by a woman. I try to be careful and restrain myself, but this is not easy. People are so ridiculous sometimes that I have to make remarks about it, even knowing afterwards that I've done something which in the long run may turn against me.

Male humorists use aggressive humor more frequently than females. They also adopt cynical positions and employ irony more frequently; women rarely do so.

In addition to the social and aggressive functions of humor, many amateurs (mostly males) use humor as a defense mechanism. The most usual form of this type of humor is self-disparagement, whose advantages were nicely expressed by one amateur humorist:

> People almost instinctively hate those who are involved in self-aggrandizing generalizations. We don't like those who try to demonstrate how intelligent, successful, and clever they are. By contrast those who can show themselves as *schlemiels* [clumsy clods] quickly gain others' sympathy. Is it because we all feel *schlemiels* deep down inside, and we admire those who can express it openly? I don't know, but I found out that people like those who can joke at their own failures and weaknesses are well liked.

One thing about humor is as clear for humorists as for nonhumorists: Humor is a trait high in social desirability. In my research, I found that when people are asked whether they have a sense of humor or not, 97% answer affirmatively. As Frank Moore Colby (1926) expressed it, "Men will confess to treason, murder, arson, false teeth or a wig. How many of them will own up to a lack of humor?" (p. 26). However, amateur humorists perceive themselves as possessing this characteristic in a higher degree than nonhumorists do. When I asked the two groups to state to what degree they would *like* to have humor, the discrepancies were significantly higher for the nonhumorists. In short, those who have a sense of humor are glad of it; those who lack it wish they had more.

Finally, I asked humorists and nonhumorists for what purposes they used humor. Their answers are graphically presented in Figure 12.3.

Let us now proceed to look into amateur humorists' personalities.

Personality

Following the personality model outlined in Chapter 9, I discuss first the cognitive dimension, then the social dimension, and finally the emotional dimension. The order we shall follow is based on the hierarchy of the three dimensions as presented in our discussion on humor creation (see pp. 143–144).

The cognitive dimension. The relationship between humor and intelligence among amateur humorists, contrary to expectations, is not a simple one. Correlations between intelligence and the results of the

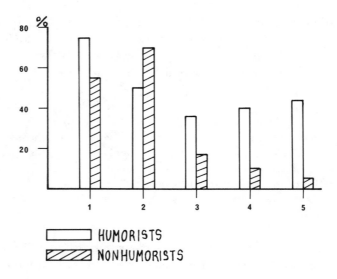

HUMORISTS
NONHUMORISTS

1. FOR A GOOD ATMOSPHERE
2. AGAINST EMBARRASSMENT
3. FOR AROUSING AFFECTION
4. FOR HURTING PEOPLE
5. FOR AMUSEMENT

FIGURE 12.3

humor tests vary from population to population. In certain groups, no correlations can be found; in others, they are low, and in still others, significant correlations emerge. This kind of variance makes one wonder about published articles that present the results obtained from relatively small groups.

One thing is certain: In none of the research groups studied was a negative correlation found between humor and intelligence. On the basis of mean correlations from more than a dozen studies involving some 1,200 adolescents and about 400 adults, some generalizations can be advanced:

1. Correlations between humor and intelligence are higher for adults than for adolescents. They are also higher for older adolescents (those aged 16–18) than for younger ones (those aged 14–15). This is probably due to the fact that adult humor in general is more sophisticated; its relation to intelligence is therefore more significant.

2. Correlations between verbal intelligence and humor are higher than those between nonverbal intelligence and humor. Since in adulthood and later adolescence most humor is verbal, these results can easily be understood.

3. Correlations between intelligence and humor creativity are higher than those between intelligence and humor appreciation. There is no doubt that creating humor is an intellectually more demanding task than simply enjoying it; this finding conforms to the hypotheses presented in the discussion of the intellectual functions of humor in Chapter 5.

4. Finally, correlations between humor and intelligence are significantly higher for males than for females. It is possible that this can be explained by the fact that the most important function of humor is the aggressive one. Males are more aggressive, and, for the more intelligent among them, humor constitutes an excellent sublimation for aggression. (The less intelligent probably use more direct forms of aggression.)

We can conclude that, in general, humorists are more intelligent than nonhumorists. However, amateur humorists as a group are far from having the high IQs found among professional humorists.

Concerning creativity, the results are clear and highly significant: Amateur humorists are more creative than nonhumorists. Humorists can see things in original and unexpected ways. They use disociation, and local logic is not strange to them. These concepts are basic for humorous as well as for creative thinking; the relationship between humor and creativity is well established. Among the many practical uses of humor, furthermore, is its value as a tool for encouraging the expression of creative ideas. In an experiment (Ziv, 1976) with adolescents, I investigated the possibility of increasing creative responses as a function of listening to humor (see Example 12.4).

Creativity, or, more precisely, divergent thinking, is the clearest cognitive trait of amateur humorists. When I investigated the part played by creativity as compared with other variables in humor, I found it to be the best predictor of humorous behavior.

The social dimension. I have noted that professional humorists, especially writers, are rather introverted. Amateurs, in contrast, are—

EXAMPLE 12.4
Humor Fostering Creativity

In order to verify the hypothesis that listening to and enjoying humor encourages the expression of creative answers, I worked with the following research design: I chose a few records by popular Israeli humorists and took them into six classrooms of 11th-graders. While they listened and laughed, the amplitude and duration of the laughter were recorded on an audiometer. The record eliciting the most laughter was chosen as a research instrument. I then worked with four different groups; two were given creativity tests of the type described in Chapter 10, and two listened to the humorous record. Afterwards, all four groups completed a parallel test of creativity.

Results clearly showed that those who had listened to the humorous record scored significantly higher on the creativity tests than those who had not. The highest difference between the two groups was obtained on the originality scores.

as a group — extroverted. As the results of self-image questionnaires have indicated, amateur humorists of both sexes perceive themselves as more sociable than nonhumorists (see Example 12.2). When administering my personality test to humorists and nonhumorists (adults as well as adolescents), I found that humorists received significantly higher scores than nonhumorists on extroversion. The typical behavior of extroverts is described in Chapter 9.

Amateur humorists spread good humor in social interactions. They feel at ease with others and enjoy being liked. Their use of humor is primarily motivated by the need for acceptance. It is certain that giving others pleasure by making them laugh increases their social status.

The social status of a person in a group can be measured using the concepts of *popularity* and *leadership*. These are related, but by no means identical. *Popularity* is the outstanding mark of the social ability to make oneself liked. In every group, there are some people whose company everyone wants and who generate a pleasant atmosphere. Studies show that popularity is a function of many variables, including a talent for easy communication, extroversion, flexibility in interpersonal relations, and a readiness to cooperate (Miller & Gentry, 1980). *Leadership* is the ability to influence and direct others in a group.

Research suggests that it is associated with self-confidence, flexibility, initiative, knowledge in areas relevant to the group's aims, and the ability to present and defend these aims.

Empirical evidence suggesting a relationship between humor and popularity has been produced by Goodchilds (1959). She found that, among adolescents, popularity is associated with the ability to laugh and to make others laugh. These qualities, among others, were mentioned by most of her subjects when she asked them what it takes to be popular. However, using the two dimensions of humor creativity and appreciation, I discovered some important differences. I found that humorists had higher popularity scores (as measured by sociometric tests) than nonhumorists. This was especially true for those who scored high on humor creativity. When I asked adolescents to nominate the most popular persons in their class, I found that such nominations were highly correlated with the ability to make others laugh, but not with the ability to laugh oneself. A popular person brings something special to the group. It seems that being able to make other group members laugh is an important contribution to the group's cohesiveness. It increases members' attraction to the group and creates a pleasurable climate.

As I have already mentioned, those who can make others laugh have a certain social power: They can influence the others' behavior. They create circumstances to which the others have to respond. This response — laughter — is a pleasurable feeling, and the humorist is therefore rewarded by receiving status in the group. Nor does creating humor in a group only bring popularity; it is also related to leadership. To my knowledge, the relationship between humor and leadership in informal groups has never been empirically investigated.

I asked adolescents, "Whom would you like to represent your class to the school administration?" Checking these results with the results on the humor measurements, I found that humorists were significantly more frequently nominated than nonhumorists. This was more true for boys than for girls, and, again, humor creativity was more strongly related than humor enjoyment to leadership (the same was true for popularity). In addition, I found that humor creation is a better predictor of leadership than intelligence. One exception to these findings was that a few adolescents who had rather high scores on humor tests were not nominated for leadership positions. Interviewing them, I found that they were what I would like to call "compulsive humorists."

This phenomenon has already been noted in relation to the behavior of some performing professionals.

Compulsive humorists are those who seem unable to stop cracking jokes, making humorous observations, and behaving like clowns. It is almost impossible to have a serious conversation with such people. Everything seems to stimulate them to humor. While they certainly contribute to a pleasant atmosphere, one gets rather tired of their continual joking. It becomes difficult to take them seriously, and this is why they are not considered leaders.

The compulsive jokester certainly has difficulty in dealing with the more serious aspects of life. His constant joking is a way of avoiding confrontation with others; one is inclined to see a defense mechanism in his behavior. His efforts to be liked and admired become pathetic, and there is no doubt that he could benefit from some form of counseling.

Amateur humorists, as a group, are therefore popular among their peers; most of them (except for compulsive humorists) are leaders and fall near the "extroversion" end of the social continuum of personality. Although they are extroverts, however, this does not mean that they are exclusively focused on relations with others. From their interviews, it appears that they have a rich inner life; they report more daydreaming and more fantasizing than nonhumorists. In their daily lives, they are not very well organized. Adult humorists reported having trouble with money because of being rather extravagant. They like money for what it can bring, more so than nonhumorists; however, they consider it less important in itself than their peers do.

The social dimension in its relation with humor has been investigated from a different angle by Shilo (1982). She compared the interest areas of humorists and nonhumorists, using Holland's (1966) test. Six types of orientation are measured by this test: realistic, intellectual, social, conventional, enterprising, and artistic. In two of these categories — the social and the artistic — humorists scored significantly higher than their nonhumorist peers. Holland describes the social orientation as being characterized by high sociability and a need for attention. The artistic orientation is characterized by introspection and a need for individualistic expression. These interests, incidentally, rank high for persons involved in education, literature, and the humanities in general.

In conclusion, most amateur humorists are extroverts who enjoy the company of others; they like to occupy center stage and to influence others. Of course, not all of them are so strongly socially oriented. Some are introverts whose humor probably fulfills more of a defensive role than a social one.

The emotional dimension. On the emotional dimension, we also find a different picture from the one arrived at for professional humorists. While the professionals are highly emotional, most amateur humorists are stable. The amateurs are generally in a good mood; anxiety and worry are alien to them. Optimistic, fun-loving *bon vivants,* amateur humorists love life and tend to be of the sanguine temperament described by Hippocrates.

It is possible that these personality traits result not only from inborn characteristics, but from family patterns characterized by good and healthy relationships. I note in Chapter 11 that conflict between the parents was frequently a part of the childhoods of professional humorists. Amateurs in my research, by contrast, talked about good family relations, with a pleasant atmosphere and playful and accepting parents. Many mentioned humorous models in their families (mostly fathers) and described the ways in which their humorous remarks were positively reinforced.

As we have seen, amateur humorists have a more positive self-image than nonhumorists. This indicates good adjustment and healthy coping abilities. On tests for anxiety, humorists had significantly lower scores than nonhumorists. Humor and anxiety involve contrary moods and feelings.

These characteristics situate amateur humorists close to the "stability" end of the emotional continuum. One possible explanation for this fact is that emotional people readily take things to heart. Stable ones do not, and this makes it easier for them to laugh at many things that would arouse worry in emotional people. Some amateur humorists are more emotional than stable, but they are definitely a minority. In general, amateur humorists are stable, well-adjusted people, with extrovert interests.

To sum up what is known from the research concerning amateur humorists, I should emphasize, as I do in Chapter 11 for professionals, that we are not dealing with a homogeneous group. Individual differences exist, and each humorist has his own personality. However, some generalizations can be made, and these are presented in Example 12.5.

Comparing these generalizations with those made about professional humorists (see Example 11.2), it is clear that we are faced with two different groups. While amateur humorists have well-adjusted personalities and are happy with those around them and with themselves, professionals are more complex. How and why some (very few) amateur humorists turn professional is an intriguing question. Future research may provide some answers.

EXAMPLE 12.5
Tentative Generalizations about Amateur Humorists

There are more male than female amateur humorists.

Female humorists see themselves less in accordance with the prevailing female sex-role stereotypes than female nonhumorists do.

Males create more humor; females enjoy it more.

The family life of amateur humorists is generally conflict-free, with good parent-child relations.

Fathers' acceptance plays a more important role in humorist girls' background; mothers' acceptance seems more important for humorist boys.

The correlation between humor and intelligence is a positive one, but it is not very strong. It is stronger for males than for females.

Humorists are more creative than their nonhumorist peers.

Extroversion is the characteristic social trait of humorists. They are involved with people, fond of social interaction, and fun-loving.

Humorists are liked by others and enjoy popularity in their groups.

Humorists have leadership traits and are more frequently nominated for such positions than nonhumorists. One exception is the compulsive humorist, who has no leadership status.

Humorists are on the stable part of the emotional continuum, and they are well adjusted.

Humorists have positive self-images, and they are less anxious and insecure than nonhumorists.

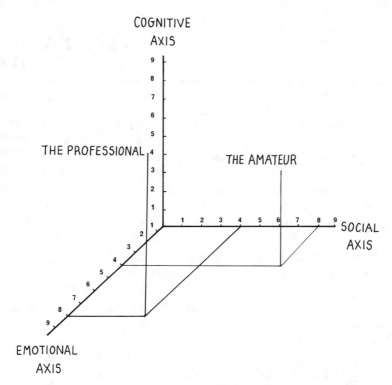

PERSONALITY DIMENSIONS : PROFESSIONALS AND AMATEURS

FIGURE 12.4

Using the personality summary system with stanines, I have produced shorthand descriptions of professional and amateur humorists:

	Intellectual	Social	Emotional
Professionals	9	4	8
Amateurs	6	8	3

These descriptions are expressed graphically in Figure 12.4.

Humorists, amateurs as well as professionals, contribute in many different ways to our lives. As Marcel Pagnol (1948) wrote, "One who can make humans laugh, who have so many reasons to weep, gives them the power to live and we love him as a benefactor."

Afterword

After all this discussion, do we understand humor better? I sincerely hope so, but I am aware that many questions remain unanswered. The explanations I have proposed for some aspects of humor are certainly not appropriate to other aspects. Humor is too complex a phenomenon to be clarified with facility. This does not mean however, that attempting to clarify it is not worth the effort. I am thoroughly aware that not everything about humor has been explained in this book, but I hope that at least some points as to the relationship between humor and personality are now clearer.

One may ask why we should try to understand humor at all. Wouldn't it be better simply to enjoy it without analysis? Perhaps. But some of us are fascinated by human behavior. Laughter is one of its most wonderful forms, and humor, which is in most cases the cause of laughter, is intriguing. Shouldn't we do our best to understand these phenomena? Certainly those of you who have had the interest and patience to read this book think so. I sincerely hope that you are not disappointed by what you have learned. But if you are, you should go on thinking, reading, and seeking more and better comprehension.

It is not only intellectual curiosity that drives some of us toward a better understanding of humor. Intuitively, most people know that humor can contribute to better human relations. Unfortunately, research demonstrating this aspect of humor is rather scarce, but it is slowly growing. Since the publication of Cousins's famous book *Anatomy of an Illness* (1979), in which he describes how laughter helped to bring him back to health from the brink of terrible illness, people in medicine have begun to investigate "the healing powers of laughter." This phrase forms the subtitle of Moody's *Laugh After Laugh* (1978). Robinson's book, *Humor and the Health Professions* (1977), investigates the contribution of humor and laughter to both patients and healers.

Education is another field in which humor has been shown to be helpful. In an earlier book, *L'Humour en Education: Approche Psychologique (Humor in Education: A Psychological Approach)* (1979a), I present a series of research projects that demonstrate how humor can raise the quality of both learning and teaching. The value of humor in improving creative thinking is also shown, and some results are briefly presented.

Practically everywhere human beings live and communicate, humor exists. Understanding it better and using it more freely can help to make our lives somewhat more enjoyable. Learning about it may be an encouragement to this end. I hope that this book will contribute a little toward such understanding.

References

Adler, A. *Understanding human nature.* New York: Premier Books, 1959.

Allport, G. W. *Personality: A psychological interpretation.* London: Constable, 1956.

Bergler, E. *Laughter and the sense of humor.* New York: International Medical Books, 1956.

Bergson, H. *Le rire.* Paris: PUF, 1975. (Originally published, 1899.)

Beyle, M. H. [Stendhal]. *Racine et Shakespeare.* Paris: Oeuvres, 1823.

Brown, T. *Anthropological studies.* London: Tait, 1925.

Buchwald, A. A conversation with *Psychology Today. Psychology Today,* 1967, pp. 14–23.

Cantor, J. R. What is funny to whom? *Journal of Communication,* 1976, *26,* 164–172.

Cantor, J. R., & Zillman, D. Resentment toward victimized protagonists and severity of misfortunes they suffer as factors in humor appreciation. *Journal of Experimental Research in Personality,* 1973, *6,* 321–329.

Cattell, R. B. *Personality and motivation: Structure and measurement.* New York: Harcourt, Brace & World, 1957.

Chaplin, C. *My autobiography.* New York: Pocket Books, 1966.

Chapman, A. J., & Gadfield, N. J. Is sexual sex sexist? *Journal of Communication,* 1967, *26,* 114–153.

Clemens, S. L. [Mark Twain]. *Notebook.* New York: Harper & Brothers, 1935.

Colby, F. M. *Satire and teeth.* New York: Macmillan, 1926.

Coser, R. L. Laughter among colleagues: A study of the social functions of humor among the staff of a mental hospital. *Psychiatry,* 1960, *23,* 81–95.

Cousins, N. *Anatomy of an illness.* New York: Norton, 1979.

Darwin, C. *The expression of the emotions in man and animals.* London: Murray, 1872.

Dearborn, G. U. N. The nature of the smile and the laugh. *Science,* 1900, *9,* 851–856.

Dollard, J., & Miller, M. *Frustration and aggression.* New Haven: Yale University Press, 1939.

Escarpit, R. *L'humour.* Paris: PUF, 1963.

Eysenck, H. J., & Eysenck, S. B. G. *Personality structure and measurement.* London: Routledge & Kegan Paul, 1969.

Festinger, L. *A theory of cognitive dissonance.* Stanford, Calif.: Stanford University Press, 1957.

Fisher, R. L., & Fisher, S. *A psychological analysis of comedians and clowns.*

Paper presented at the Third International Conference on Humor, Washington, D.C., 1982.

Foot, H. C., & Chapman, A. J. The social responsiveness of young children in humorous situations. In A. J. Chapman & H. C. Foot (Eds.), *Humor and laughter: Theory, research and application.* London: Wiley, 1976.

France, A. *L'île des pinguins.* Paris: Hachette, 1931.

Freud, S. *[Jokes and their relation to the unconscious.]* New York: Moffat Ward, 1916. (Originally published, 1905.)

Freud, S. [Contributions to the psychology of love: The most prevalent form of degradation in erotic life.] In S. Freud, *Collected papers* (Vol. 4) (J. Strachey, Ed. and trans.). New York: Basic Books, 1959. (Originally published, 1912.)

Freud, S. [Humor.] In S. Freud, *Collected papers* (Vol. 4) (J. Strachey, Ed. and trans.). New York: Basic Books, 1959. (Originally published, 1928.)

Frigyes, K. *Igy irtok ti.* Budapest: Nagy, 1937.

Fry, W. F. Jr. Psychodynamics of sexual humor: Women's view of sex. *Medical Aspects of Human Sexuality,* 1972, *6,* 136–139.

Fry, W. F., & Allen, M. *Make 'em laugh.* Palo Alto, Calif.: Science and Behavior Books, 1975.

Gerwitz, J. L. The course of infant smiling in four child rearing environments in Israel. In B. M. Foss (Ed.), *Determinants of infant behavior* (Vol. 3). London: Methuen, 1965.

Getzels, J. W., & Jackson, P. W. *Creativity and intelligence: Explorations with gifted children.* New York: Wiley, 1962.

Goertzel, V., & Goertzel, F. *Cradles of eminence.* Boston: Little, Brown, 1962.

Goodchilds, G. D. Effects of being witty on position in the social structure of a small group. *Sociometry,* 1959, *22,* 261–272.

Greenberg, D. *How to be a Jewish mother.* New York: Price Stern Sloan, 1965.

Gregory, J. C. *The nature of laughter.* London: Kegan Paul, 1924.

Grotjahn, M. *Beyond laughter: Humor and the subconscious.* New York: McGraw-Hill, 1966.

Gruner, C. R. *Understanding laughter: The workings of wit and humor.* Chicago: Nelson Hall, 1978.

Guilford, J. P. Three faces of intellect. *American Psychologist,* 1959, *19,* 469–479.

Haning, P. *The Hollywood nightmare.* London: McDonald, 1970.

Harter, C. Children's problem solving behavior. *Experimental Child Psychology,* 1974, *7,* 143–151.

Hasset, J., & Houlihan, J. Different jokes for different folks. *Psychology Today,* 1979, pp. 64–68.

Heller, J. *Catch-22.* New York: Simon & Schuster, 1961.

Highet, G. *The anatomy of satire.* Princeton, N.J.: Princeton University Press, 1954.

Hobbes, T. *Leviathan.* London: Grooke, 1650.

Holland, J. L. *The psychology of vocational choice.* Waltham, Mass.: Blaisdell, 1966.

Huxley, A. *Control of the mind*. London: Farber & Wilson, 1961.

Hyghet, A. B. *Satire*. London: Macmillan, 1959.

Janus, S. S. The great comedians: Personality and other factors. *American Journal of Psychoanalysis*, 1975, *35*, 169–174.

Kagan, J. *Change and continuity in infancy*. New York: Wiley, 1971.

Klingman, A. *[Preference of boys from different upbringings for two counseling approaches.]* Unpublished doctoral dissertation, Tel Aviv University, 1978. (Hebrew)

Koestler, A. *The act of creation*. London: Hutchinson Press, 1964.

Lax, E. *On being funny: Woody Allen and comedy*. New York: Charterhouse, 1975.

Leacock, S. B. *Humor and humanity*. London: John Lane, 1935.

Levine, J. B. The feminine routine. *Journal of Communication*, 1976, *26*, 173–175.

Levin, K., Lippit, R., & White, R. An experimental study of leadership and group life. In E. E. Maccoby, T. M. Newcomb, & E. L. Hartley (Eds.), *Readings in social psychology*. New York: Holt, Rinehart & Winston, 1958.

Lewis, J. *Film making*. New York: Random House, 1962.

Lorenz, K. *On aggression*. New York: Harcourt, 1963.

Losco, J., & Epstein, S. Humor preference as a subtle measure of attitudes toward the same and the opposite sex. *Journal of Personality*, 1975, *43*, 321–334.

Martineau, W. H. A model of the social functions of humor. In J. H. Goldstein & P. E. McGhee (Eds.), *The psychology of humor*. New York: Academic Press, 1972.

Mauldin, B. *Up front*. New York: Bantam Books, 1945.

McDougall, W. The nature of laughter. *Nature*, 1903, *67*, 318–319.

McGhee, P. E. *Humor: Its origin and development*. New York: Freeman, 1979.

McGhee, P. E., & Chapman, A. J. *Children's humor*. New York: Wiley, 1980.

Meryman, R. Carol Burnett's own story. *McCall's*, February 1978, p. 76.

Mikes, G. *Humor: In memoriam*. London: Routledge & Kegan Paul, 1970.

Miller, N., & Gentry, K. W. Sociometric indices of children's peer interaction in the school setting. In H. C. Foot, A. J. Chapman, & J. R. Smith (Eds.), *Friendship and social relations in children*. New York: Wiley, 1980.

Mindess, H. *The chosen people?* Los Angeles: Nash Publications, 1972.

Mishkinsky, M. Humor as a "courage mechanism." *Israeli Annals of Psychiatry and Related Disciplines*, 1977, *15*, 352–365.

Moody, R. A. *Laugh after laugh: The healing power of humor*. Jacksonville, Fla.: Headwaters, 1978.

Nevo, O. *Humor responses as an expression of aggression by Jews and Arabs in Israel*. Jerusalem: Hebrew University Doctoral Dissertation, 1980 (Hebrew).

Norman, W. T. Toward an adequate taxonomy of personality attributes: Replicated factor structure in peer nomination personality ratings. *Jour-*

nal of Abnormal and Social Psychology, 1963, *66,* 574–583.

Oakley, A. *Sex, gender, and society.* New York: Harper & Row, 1972.

Obrdlik, A. J. Gallows humor: A sociological phenomenon. *American Journal of Sociology,* 1942, *47,* 71–74.

O'Connell, W. E. Creativity in humor. *Journal of Social Psychology,* 1969, *78,* 237–241.

Odbert, H. S., & Allport, G. W. Trait-names: A psycho-lexical study. *Psychological Monographs,* 1936, *47*(Whole No. 211).

Pagnol, M. *Le rire et la comedie.* Paris: Meridian, 1948.

Pannenbourg, W. A. *Les écrivains satiriques.* Paris: PUF, 1954.

Penjon, R. Humour et liberté. *Revue Philosophique,* 1893, *12,* 42–71.

Piaget, J. *Plays, dreams and imitation in childhood.* London: Macmillan, 1951.

Pollio, H. R., & Edgerly, J. Comedians and comic styles. In A. J. Chapman & H. C. Foot (Eds.), *Humor and laughter: Theory, research and application.* London: Wiley, 1976.

Radcliffe-Brown, A. R. On joking relationships. *Africa,* 1940, *13,* 195–210.

Rapp, A. A phylogenetic theory of wit and humor. *Journal of Social Psychology,* 1949, *30,* 81–96.

Reik, T. Freud and Jewish wit. *Psychoanalysis,* 1954, *5,* 13–28.

Robinson, V. R. *Humor and the health professions.* Thorofare, N.J.: Charles Slack, 1977.

Rouff, L. L. Creativity and sense of humor. *Psychological Reports,* 1975, *37,* 1022.

Sauvy, B. *Humour et politique.* Paris: Flamarion, 1979.

Schachter, S., & Wheeler, L. Epinephrine, chlorpromazine and amusement. *Journal of Abnormal and Social Psychology,* 1962, *65,* 121–128.

Schaeffer, E. S. Children's reports of parental behavior: An inventory. *Child Development,* 1965, *36,* 413–424.

Sherman, L. W. An ecological study of glee in small groups of preschool children. *Child Development,* 1975, *46,* 53–61.

Shilo, S. *[Humor creation: Its relationship to individual and situational characteristics.]* Unpublished doctoral dissertation, Tel Aviv University, 1982. (Hebrew)

Shurcliff, A. Judged humor, arousal and the relief theory. *Journal of Personality and Social Psychology,* 1968, *8,* 360–363.

Spencer, H. The physiology of laughter. *Macmillan's Magazine,* 1860, *1,* 395–402.

Taylor, C. W., & Baron, F. *Scientific creativity: Its recognition and development.* New York: Wiley, 1963.

Torrance, E. P. *The Torrance Test of Creative Thinking.* Lexington, Mass.: Ginn, 1974.

Watson, J. B. *Behaviorism.* New York: Worton, 1930.

Weiss, L. L'humour juif—Approche philosophique. *Revue de Philosophie,* 1952, *87,* 56–81.

Ziv, A. *Children's need for anxiety.* Tel Aviv University, 1973 (Hebrew).

Ziv, A. The effects of humor on creativity. *Journal of Educational Psychology,* 1976, *3,* 318–322.

Ziv, A. *Counselling and the intellectually gifted child.* Toronto: Toronto University Press, 1977.

Ziv, A. *L'humour en education: Approche psychologique.* Paris: ESF, 1979. (a)

Ziv, A. Sociometry of humor: Objectifying the subjective. *Perceptual and Motor Skills,* 1979, *49,* 97–98. (b)

Ziv, A. *[Psychology of humor.]* Tel Aviv: Yahdav, 1980. (Hebrew)

Ziv, A. The self concept of adolescent humorists. *Journal of Adolescence,* 1981, *4,* 187–197.

Ziv, A. The influence of humorous atmosphere on divergent thinking. *Contemporary Educational Psychology,* 1983, *8,* 413–421.

Ziv, A., Rimon, J., & Doni, M. Parental perception and self concept of gifted and average underachievers. *Perceptual and Motor Skills,* 1977, *44,* 563–568.

Index

Index

183